On Beating the Market

How to Profit Where Others Have Failed

William John Bignell

About On Beating the Market

Have you heard that bonds are safer than stocks? That's true... except when it's not.

Or that gold is the best way to hedge against a bear market? True again... except when it's not.

In this easy-to-follow breakdown of the fundamentals of equity investment, Bill Bignell investigates many of the common strategies (and misconceptions) of investors in today's market, offering plenty of anecdotes, mini case studies and a selection of revealing graphs to make a compelling case. Using comparisons between the Canadian and US stock markets, Bill shows some interesting trends... and busts some entrenched myths in the process.

With chapters on the various ways of accessing financial markets (including analyses on the pros and cons of various options such as mutual funds and exchange traded funds), the right and wrong ways to time the market, diversification and the most important metrics to keep an eye on when you invest, On Beating the Market is a must-have introduction to the intricacies of equity investing, laid out in plain language so that even a layperson will understand.

E. J. Clarke – Silver Jay Editing

On Beating the Market

Introduction

Is investing on your own really that difficult? Is it true that stocks are better in the long run? What about bonds? Why do mutual funds never seem to keep up with market averages? Which approach is more likely to beat the market - growth or value? Is it even possible to beat the market?

There are some 25,000 Investment Advisors in Canada and 75,000 mutual fund salespersons (many of whom are Certified Financial Planners and many who just call themselves Financial Planners). Every one of them has an opinion for each of these questions, and it is entirely possible that no two will be the same. Yet every one of them can point to some report or study that supports their view.

Eugene Famma and Harry Markowitz have won Nobel Prizes for arguing that stock markets are so efficient they always reflect the true value of their constituent companies, so no-one can consistently beat them. Robert Schiller and Daniel Kahneman have won Nobel Prizes for explaining why markets are often mis-priced, and that they can be beaten. There are growth managers and value managers. There are managers who describe their style as "Growth at a Reasonable Price".

Some believe strongly in the Efficient Markets Theory and claim the only thing you need to do is buy Exchange Traded Funds that mimic the market. At the other extreme, market technicians theorize that because people have short memories, they tend to make the same mistakes time and time again. So they study stock charts, looking for patterns they hope to exploit in order to make profits.

Still others hold that every company has some intrinsic value which, if identified, can serve as a guide to the price an investor should be willing to pay in order to purchase stock in that company. Now we're talking some sense! This is the approach practiced by Value Investors. Unfortunately, there is not universal agreement among value investors as to how to arrive at that intrinsic value.

Analysts measure cash flow, earnings growth, annual sales, return on invested capital, return on equity, book value, quick ratios, P/E ratios, earnings margin, dividend pay-out ratios, etcetera, etcetera, etcetera. There are literally dozens of ratios which are studied and analysed by investment gurus and practitioners. Some feel this or that group of ratios is most important while others prefer another mix. And there is no agreement on what level of this or that constitutes cheap or expensive. No wonder the average investor has trouble making sense of it all!

Over my thirty-plus years in the investment industry, I survived the effects of the 1987 market crash, the Mexican currency crisis, the Russian debt default, the "Asian Contagion" as well as the implosion of the tech bubble and the financial crisis of 2008. Along the way, I studied the "conventional wisdom", tried a number of strategies, learned from some celebrated experts and found that convention isn't always so wise.

I found that by following a disciplined value-oriented approach and sticking with one's plan while avoiding the influence of every-day market gyrations and flavour-of-the-month strategies that come and go like a passing carnival, it is indeed possible to beat the market over the longer term. I was able to do just that for my client base over several years, and on the pages that follow, I will explain how you, too, can beat the market.

Acknowledgements

As with any work of this nature, it's always great to have a little help from your friends. I would like to thank Brian Wadsworth as well as Mike Peters, both of Industrial Alliance Securities for their insights and helpful comments. I would also like to thank EJ Clarke of Silver Jay Editing for her valuable contributions.

And finally, my gratitude goes out to my wife, Nancy for her support and patience while I undertook this project.

Table of Contents:

Chapter 1

Starting with Your Investment Profile

You've decided it's time to open an investment account, or to move your existing assets to a different institution, and the first thing your new financial advisor is going to do is have you fill out a questionnaire. Generally, this entails a series of questions designed to assess your tolerance for risk, your time horizon, and income requirements, and to help choose the kind of portfolio best suited to you.

Here are a few of the things you will be asked to consider:

Liquidity:

Many Financial Planners advocate having an amount equal to 3 to 6 months' family expenses available in cash or equivalent at all times, in case of some emergency. Maintaining liquidity means holding part of your portfolio in cash or some other investment which is readily convertible into cash on short notice without penalty. This could be Government Treasury Bills, short-term bank certificates or a money market fund.

There are also times when you may have sold off other assets (stocks, bonds etc.) because they became too pricey, and you have not yet found a suitable replacement investment. And that might not be so bad because it comes in handy to have a cash reserve to take advantage of the markets after they have sold off and are poised to start heading back up.

Income Needs:

Typically, investment advisors will recommend you structure your investment portfolio depending on your need for income. If you are retired and depend on your investments to subsidize your pension income, they will no doubt suggest you focus on bonds and high dividend-paying equities. A younger investor, willing to assume more risk might be pointed to more growth-oriented stocks or funds and more aggressive investment strategies.

You will discover as you continue reading, however, that these more aggressive strategies and investments tend to under-perform solid, high-value, dividend paying equities over time. If you are investing for the entertainment value, by all means buy momentum stocks, follow high growth/high-risk strategies, and have fun. But if what you really want is reliable, long-term performance, I always recommend investing like you want/need dividend income.

Time Horizon:

Your time horizon is also a critical factor in deciding on how to structure your investments. If you have no near or intermediate term needs for the money you have invested, you are better able to assume the risk of a more volatile portfolio, knowing that if the market or a particular stock turns down temporarily, you will be able to wait it out, provided the long-term prospects are favorable. But always remember that markets can be unpredictable, and if you will need to cash out part or all of your portfolio in the near or mid-term, you should not be invested in securities that go up and down in price (see liquidity).

Risk Tolerance:

What is risk anyway, and how do we go about defining it? Most people if asked would define investment risk as the chance of losing their money. Sounds simple, but there is more to risk than meets the eye. Risk is generally defined as:

> *The chance that an investment's actual return will be different than expected. Risk includes the possibility of losing some or all of the original investment. Different versions of risk are usually measured by calculating the standard deviation of the historical returns or average returns of a specific investment. A high standard deviation indicates a high degree of risk.* [1]

Standard deviation is a measure of volatility, and it is how conventional wisdom defines risk. Not necessarily the odds of losing all your money, but rather the chances your rate of return will be something other than the average. So, if your return is above average, conventional wisdom is that it must be risky.

While I do not question that a history of ever-changing returns usually suggests a risky investment, I do ask "Is that the definitive and only thing you should consider when evaluating risk?" Certainly not! Two issues I have with conventional analysis are that things like risk and volatility are generally measured using data that often goes back more than a hundred years, and there is no distinction made between cause and effect.

If one were to make a list ranking automobiles according to the fewest accidents for each 1,000 cars sold over the last 100 years, I expect cars like Volvo would be at or near the top, while cars like Ferrari and similar sporty models would be near the bottom. Should this reflect poorly on the manufacturer of Ferrari automobiles and well on Volvo? Truthfully, I have no data that suggests a Ferrari is built any more or less safe than a Volvo, but I do suspect most drivers who buy Ferraris do so for the thrill, and the speed the sports-car offers. Volvo drivers, I suspect, are really just looking for reliable transportation.

What happens if we turn the tables? Suppose I crank my shiny new Volvo up as fast as I can make it go and run it up a mountain road with twists and turns, and a 900-foot drop- six feet from the shoulder of the road? Is my risk level low because I am driving a Volvo?

And suppose you get in your Ferrari, start the engine and take a nice leisurely drive around the countryside, observing all speed limits and traffic signs. Are you being more risky because you are driving a Ferrari? One hundred years of statistics might suggest you are, but that's not the way I see it.

Any investment involves risk. If you invest in real estate, you run the risk of land values collapsing, having bad tenants or of your building needing unexpected repairs. If you invest in Guaranteed Investment Certificates you run the risk of interest rates increasing just after you locked in for five years. Conversely, if you invest in Government Treasury-bills, there is a risk the rates will go down significantly, and you wishing you had locked in.

Perhaps more important is the issue of timeline. As noted above, many financial statistics are compared to over 100 years of data. No account is made of business cycles, interest rate cycles or the significant changes in technology that have occurred in that time. In the 1970's, several middle-eastern countries banded together and flexed their newly-found economic muscle by imposing an oil embargo on the rest of the world.

This helped drive inflation up to record levels which, in turn, drove interest rates up into the 20% range in the early 1980's at the expense of bond-holders. This historic rise in interest rates took 30 years to unwind, and not only did bonds perform exceptionally well, they outperformed equities. Now, with near-zero interest rates many economists and analysts (myself included) believe this trend will be reversed before long.

Old school advisors will suggest you break down your portfolio into a series of asset classes depending on these needs and risk tolerance. It is highly likely the asset classes the recommend will include:

- Cash & Equivalents (Treasury bills, money market funds)
- Bonds
- Stocks

with the percentage allocated to each assets class dependent on your level of risk tolerance.

Again, here is where convention isn't always so wise. Because of the over-reliance on data and averages going back over 100 years, no consideration is given to the changing interest rate cycle or a plethora of asset types that didn't even exist 100 years ago.

A modern portfolio strategy should not be restricted to holding to a specific range of exclusionary asset mix classes like cash/bonds/stocks. Rather it should offer a balance of assets you feel comfortable with, and which is designed to attain your goals, and accommodate any restrictions you may have. And it should recognize that some assets classes (equities in particular) can satisfy the goals of more than one of the investment objectives of growth, income, and safety of capital.

Today's portfolio may consist of some or all of the following asset classes:

- Low-risk, highly liquid assets: Treasury bills, money market funds, bank term deposits and other short-term instruments. These assets provide liquidity, and protection from market losses, but the returns are likely to be very minimal – and likely won't even offset inflation.

- Medium-risk income-producing securities: This may include not only bonds, but also convertible securities, preferred shares and/or blue chip common shares that pay high dividends. These securities allow the investor to generate income, while mitigating some market volatility.

- Moderate to Higher-risk securities: These will likely include non-speculative, growth-oriented common stock or mutual funds or even high-risk bonds.

- Speculative Higher-risk securities: These may include (but is not restricted to) speculative penny stocks, options, warrants, hedge funds short-selling and other aggressive trading strategies.

Some more progressive investment firms have begun to view portfolio structure more in line with this second approach. It certainly makes more sense to identify assets types by what they have to offer and how they react to market forces than a hard and fast legal definition.

The chapters that follow review some more recent history of how many of these assets have fared, as well as assessing some advantages and disadvantages of owning them to point you in the direction of beating the market.

Chapter 2

Choosing your Asset Mix: The Case for Equities

In September of 2002, North American stock markets were in the middle of a nasty bear market, and the Dow was hovering around 7500. Bill Gross, co-founder of PIMCO Investment Management, and whose bond mutual fund had become so popular he earned the nick-name "The Bond King" wrote an article entitled "Dow 5500". Gross estimated that even after having fallen nearly 35% in just over a year, the fundamentals warranted another 27% decline. [1]

History shows that the Dow bottomed at 7286 a few months after Gross' report, and climbed 47% to 10737 by February 2004. [2]

On July 31, 2012, after the S&P 500 had rallied nearly 100% from its bottom in March of 2009, Gross wrote that the steady 6.5% "consistent annual returns" equity investors have enjoyed since 1912 are a thing of the past. His reasoning was that, since GDP tends to grow at around 3.5% annually over time; any stock market growth above this level means that stockholders must be: "skimming 3.0% off the top much like a chain letter or, yes - Ponzi scheme.", and that shareholders have been "consistently profiting at the expense of others." [3]

Well, let's consider that thought. Gross Domestic Product (GDP) is the measure of everything earned (or spent) by all the components of an economy combined. This includes consumers, business and government. Earnings from each of these sectors is calculated and added together. The end result is then adjusted for imports and exports to come up with the overall earnings or production of the economy.

The stockholders Mr. Gross refers to are the owners of the business sector of the overall economy – the ones Mr. Gross accuses of "skimming 3.0% off the top". They represent about 14% of GDP in the US and about 25% in Canada. Consumers represent about 68% in the US and 54% in Canada. Government spending accounts for just over 18% of US GDP and 21% in Canada.[4]

So, the question then is: "Should business earn a better return than the other two sectors of the economy?" Well, first of all, governments don't make money. They extract it from other economic sectors by way of taxation, and they spend it. To be sure, schools, roads and hospitals are necessities in a civilized society, but for the most part, government-owned institutions do not make profits – in fact, it is fair to say that government's contribution to national profits is actually negative. By any definition, a business must earn a premium over this in order to survive.

Now let's consider how businesses (shareholders) make their profits. They put up some capital; perhaps borrow more from the bank (or issue bonds), purchase some buildings and machinery, then hire employees (who also just happen to be the consumer segment of the economy) to produce the computers, cars or iPhones they hope to sell.

It would be fair to say that businesses would not borrow from the bank or issue bonds to raise capital if they did not expect to make a better return than the interest they are paying. It would be foolish to do otherwise. And it would also be fair to say that those same businesses would not hire employees (the consumers) unless they could earn a return on their production in excess of the wages they pay to those employees. (Some companies have tried this in the past– It doesn't work very well!)

I would, therefore, conclude that if business (and its shareholders) did NOT earn profits in excess of GDP growth, they would eventually cease to exist, and along with them, society as we know it today.

It would seem that what Mr. Gross is really referring to in his somewhat unflattering analogy, is what is known as the "Equity Risk Premium". This is the excess return that an individual stock or the overall stock market provides over other investment options such as bonds or treasury bills. This higher rate of return is required to entice investors to take on perceived higher risk of the equity market.

Even though he admits in his dissertation that: "Common sense would argue that appropriately priced stocks should return more than bonds. Their dividends are variable, their cash flows less certain and therefore, an equity risk premium should exist which compensates stockholders for their junior position in the capital structure." It would appear he feels this premium is too high and likely to decline.

In his epic book, "Stocks for the Long Run", Dr. Jeremy Siegel, a professor at Wharton School of Business traced returns for a number of asset classes in the US all the way back to 1802. According to Dr. Siegel, US stocks provided an average annual return of 8.1% over that period compared to 5.1% for bonds, 4.2% for Short-term Treasury Bills and just 2.1% for gold.₅

One dollars worth of gold in 1802 was worth $86.40 at the end of 2012. The same dollar put into T-Bills, and continuously re-invested would have been worth $5,379, and that number for bonds would be $33,922. Had it been invested in stocks, and the dividends re-invested, the value would be a whopping $13.48 million at the end of 2012! Dr. Siegel's work certainly tends to confirm Mr. Gross' observation that over the long term, stocks have indeed outperformed bonds – as well as most other assets. Even after factoring out inflation, stocks have produced an annualized real return of 6.6% since 1802.

Data provided by Nobel Laureate Dr. Robert Schiller, in his book "Irrational Exuberance" shows that the average Price to Earnings multiple for the S&P 500 has been 15.48 times since 1871. If a stock is trading on the market at $30.00 per share, and the company's last earnings report indicated it made a profit of $3.00 per share over the last 12 months, it has an earnings multiple (or P/E ratio) of 10 times earnings. Likewise, if a stock traded at the same $30.00 per share, but the company earned only $2.00 per share, it would have an earnings multiple of 15 times - which as we see, is about the long-term average for the market as a whole.₆

The P/E ratio is probably the most frequently quoted statistic about stocks by both laymen, and professional investors alike. So much so, that investors should be careful not to fall into too much of a casual dependence on the statistic – at least for near-term investment decisions. This will be discussed in a later section.

A review of this long-term average P/E of 15.48, however, can be very illuminating. The inversion of this number (that is - E/P, instead of P/E) is 0.0646, or 6.46%, and is known as the earnings yield. The earnings yield represents the net return to shareholders based on the total equity capitalization of a firm, whether it is paid out in dividends, or re-invested back into the company. It is also remarkably close to the real return for stocks since 1802, and with real equity returns at 6%, I am left to wonder just where are these "excess returns" that has some detractors so concerned.

There is nothing like a good look at history to get your bearings straight in the wonderful world of investments. After all, as philosopher George Santayana once wrote: "Those who cannot remember the past are condemned to repeat it."[7]

The problem now is that markets, like the economy itself, tend to fluctuate. The following graph illustrates the annual returns for the S&P 500 Index, 10 year US Treasury Bonds and 1 Year T-Bills back to 1982. Even though the S&P 500 Index has provided 8.1% annual returns for over 200 years, there is not one year depicted on this chart for which the return was exactly 8.1%.

In fact, the average S&P 500 return after dividends between 1982 and 2001 was actually 12.7%. There were 13 years when the index lost ground, the worst being 2009, at 34.6%. The best gain was 37.7% in 1996. In all, there were 13 years in which the gain exceeded 20%, yet there were 13 of the 31 years when returns were negative.[8]

Chart 2.1

Annual Returns

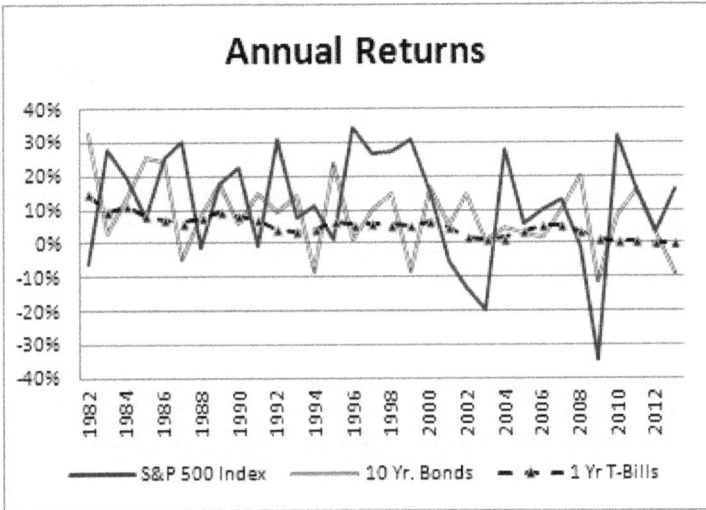

Legend: S&P 500 Index — 10 Yr. Bonds — 1 Yr T-Bills

Treasury Bonds, on the other hand, provided an average 9.5% return during the 31-year span. The best year for 10 year US Treasuries was 1982 when they provided a 32.8% return. Bonds returned more than 20% six times in the 31 year period while recording 9 losing years.

One year US Treasury Bills (a Treasury Bill is issued for a term of one year or less. A Treasury Bond is issued for a duration exceeding one year), which had peaked in 1982 at 17.63%, gradually declined throughout the ensuing 30 years, to 0.11% at the end of 2012, and sat at 0.15% at the end of 2013. Ten-year bond yields peaked in 1983 at 14.6% and worked their way down to 1.9% at year-end 2013.

The above chart illustrates that like stocks, bonds too, can be quite volatile (though admittedly, they have not been as volatile as stocks); and like stocks, they can sometimes throw off negative returns. This becomes a problem for investors during periods of rising interest rates.

Looking at the same data from a different perspective, we come up with cumulative returns for each asset class. This time, I included data from Canadian markets as well. Again, I traced asset values back to 1982, through to year-end 2014. The results were much as I expected. The value at the end of 2014 of $100 invested for each asset at the beginning of 1982 is as follows:[9]

Table 1a

S&P 500 Total Return	$3,804
US Long-term Bonds	$1,981
US 91 day T-Bills	$ 386
S&P TSX Total Return	$1,739
Canadian LT Bonds	$1,703
Canadian 91 day T-Bills	$ 609

On an annual basis, US bonds returned 10.1%, and the S&P 500 averaged 12.5%. Cumulatively, US stocks provided nearly double the return of 10 year US Treasuries. The question becomes: "Are these returns warranted? Or, have equity investors, as Mr. Gross suggested been getting a free ride?"

The Canadian indices tell a somewhat different story. While equities still out-paced bonds, the difference was marginal. Canadian stocks returned approximately 10.0% annually during the period compared to 9.6% for bonds. I have charted the Canadian and US stock returns, along with Canadian bonds and T-Bills in the following graph:

Chart 2.2

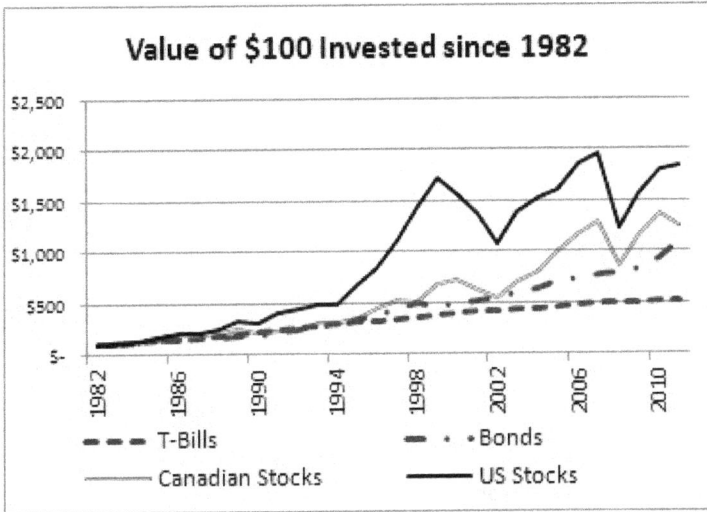

Value of $100 Invested since 1982

Source: Standard & Poor's; Scotia Capital: Federal Reserve of St. Louis; Stats Canada

Again, we can see how Canadian equities fared significantly less well than their US counterparts, and Canadian bonds nearly matched the TSX Composite Index for return. Why the difference? Should investors just buy US equities- forsaking Canadian stocks altogether? I don't think so. There are a couple of specific reasons for the underperformance in Canadian securities in recent years.

First off there was a significant decline in the value of the US dollar. Stock and bond market indices are generally quoted in domestic currencies.[11] The average value of a US dollar in 1982 was $123.34 Canadian. So, what has happened since then?

To start with, Canada's fiscal position has improved significantly in the last 30 years, in both absolute terms, and relative to other countries. As well, Quebecers seem much less inclined toward separation – or "Sovereignty Association" in the 2010's than they were in the 1980's and 1990's. And in more recent years, the US Federal Reserve aggressively expanded the US money supply, implementing "quantitative easing" in order to bolster their struggling economy. This action alone would result in a downward bias on the USD. The collective effect of these factors was to see the USD decline in value to $1.03 in 2013.[12]

That is a 16.5% decline in the value of the US Dollar, and it means that the implied $3,335 value of the S&P 500 investment in US Dollars was really worth $2,785 in Canadian Dollars. Still more than the TSX provided, but certainly lower than the nominal USD return.

In late 2013 the US began to "taper" its extraordinary monetary stimulus. This tapering carried on throughout 2014, and in 2015, the quantitative easing programme ended. And as inflation becomes more of a concern, US interest rates will eventually begin to rise. This return to more neutral US monetary policy has already eased the pressure on the Canadian dollar. Canadian exporters are now hoping this negates (or perhaps even reverses) the effect foreign exchange has played on Canadian capital markets.

The other major contributor to the lower returns in Canada, has been a lower productivity level in the Canadian labour force, and, therefore, lower corporate profits in Canada. Labour productivity is defined by Statistics Canada as real gross domestic product (GDP) per hour worked, and ours has been falling behind other major economies for several decades.

A study by The Conference Board of Canada in 2012 showed Canada's level of labour productivity was US$42; much lower than that of the United States, at US$52, and has fallen to 80 percent of the U.S. level from a high of 91 percent in the mid-1980s. In fact, Canada placed a disappointing 13th among its 16 peer countries in this area of comparison.[13] One does not need to pour over the myriad of available research to understand that low productivity will lead to lower income, exports and standard of living. But what can be done about it?

Improving productivity is not about working longer or harder; it's about working smarter. It's about finding more efficient and effective ways to produce goods and services so that more can be produced with the same amount of effort. The primary way to accomplish this goal is through capital investment.

It only makes sense that companies which utilize newer machinery and production methods should be more efficient than those that get by using decades-old machines. But a quick glance at the following chart shows that investing in machinery and equipment has not grown much in Canada in recent years; and has, in fact, declined since 2008.[14]

Chart 2.3

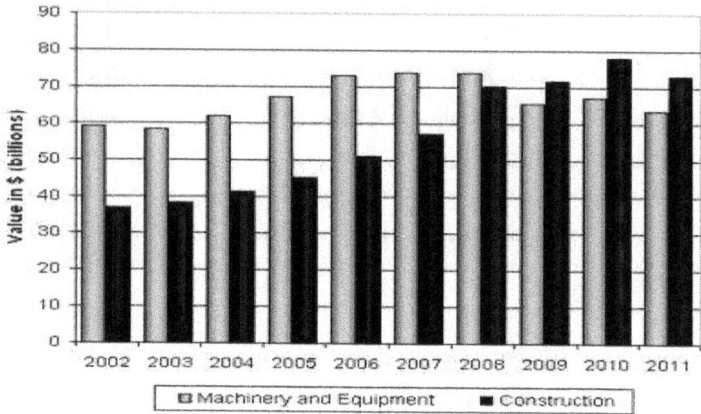

Fortunately, Canadian legislators seem to have tuned into the issue. In recent years, the government has increased its own spending on research and development, accelerated capital depreciation for manufacturing and equipment for companies, and reduced the overall tax rate for corporations by some 10%. Business has reacted and has begun to increase spending on capital investment.

After seeing an improving trend in 2013, Statistics Canada reports significant increases in intended capital investments for 2014. Manufacturers reported a 4.7% increase in investment intentions to $18.9 billion, led primarily by the petroleum and coal, chemical, and transportation equipment industries. Spending on capital machinery and equipment is anticipated to increase by 3.9% to $112 billion. It is essential that this trend continue, if Canadians hope to reclaim their place as leaders in the global economy. And assuming it continues, Canadian companies and stock markets should benefit.

18

At the end of 2014, both the S&P 500 in New York, and Toronto's S&P TSX Composite Index were reasonably priced by long-term as well as medium-term standards, although I suggest using caution if you are trying to predict short-term movements.

To sum things up, equities have provided superior returns over the years, and while stock markets have their ups and downs, so, too have other markets like bonds, commodities and real estate. American stocks have out-performed their Canadian brethren in recent years, but that is not always so. This also helps make a case for spreading your assets among different equity markets, which is discussed in more detail my chapter on diversification.

Chapter 3

Alternatives to Equities

Bonds:

Any discussion about bonds as an investment necessitates a brief overview of the kind of tools a government or its central bank has at its disposal with which it hopes to influence things like inflation, unemployment and overall economic activity.

Governments regularly utilize Fiscal Policy as a means of reducing unemployment and increasing overall economic activity. Fiscal Policy is the use by governments of adjusting taxes and spending levels in order to influence the economy. By increasing their spending, and taking on additional debt (running a fiscal budget deficit) governments hope to create demand for goods and services, thus increasing overall economic activity. This strategy was promoted vigorously during the 1930's by John Maynard Keynes as a way to end the great depression.

Of course, Keynes also recommended running budget surpluses when the economy is growing well in order to pay off the accumulated debt and balance the books. Unfortunately, this part of the plan is unpopular with the general public, and governments who curtail spending and attempt to achieve fiscal balance usually become unpopular and end up getting voted out in favour of a more free-spending party.

The other main economic tool is known as Monetary Policy, and is generally exercised by a country's central bank (ie: The

Bank of Canada). If the central bank hopes to reduce unemployment, it may reduce short-term interest rates, which tends to influence longer term interest rates. This action is generally associated with an increase in the supply of money circulating within the economy. (The central bank controls the printing presses that print the dollars you and I carry around in our wallets.)

A Low interest rates and high monetary growth strategy is known by various terms. The central bank may refer to it as "accommodative monetary policy". The press may call it "easy" or "loose" monetary policy. Critics of "loose" monetary policy point to historic evidence that it leads to inflation. Higher interest rates and slower monetary growth is called "tight" monetary policy.

With more money available, and with lower loan interest rates, people are more likely to borrow for that new car which helps encourage economic growth. If the Bank is concerned over increasing inflation, it may reduce the money supply and increase interest rates. In order to fine-tune its strategies, central banks rank money and monetary assets according to their liquidity; from M1 (the most liquid) all the way to M4 (the least liquid). The monetary definitions we are most interested in are M1 and M2.

M1 is the narrowest definition of money in Canada and consists of all currency (bills and coins) as well as chequing account deposits. M2 is the next most liquid monetary definition after M1, and includes M1 + personal savings deposits + non-personal notice deposits.

The reason this all is so important to bond investors is that when the monetary policy is loose, interest rates go down, and price levels of existing bonds go up. When monetary policy tightens, interest rates go up, and existing bond prices go down.

Looking back to chart 1-b, we can make several observations. One is that for 31 years, the cumulative returns on Canadian stocks were not appreciably better than bond returns. Secondly, as was the case in the US marketplace, stocks proved to be more volatile than bonds. Investors can hardly be blamed for feeling that perhaps they would be better off just putting their money in bonds, and forgetting about the equity market. But, let's not be too hasty.

Since bond markets have been less volatile, bonds are perceived to be less risky than stocks. Even if true it does not mean they are not risky. The main sources of risk are Default Risk and Interest Rate Risk. Default risk, as the name suggests is the risk that the bond issuer is unable to pay out interest as agreed, or to redeem the bond for cash at maturity. Interest rate risk is the risk that market interest rates may go up after you purchased your bond. This tends to devalue the cash-flow you receive and reduce the market value of your bond.

When General Motors went bankrupt in 2009 after defaulting on $27 Billion in unsecured debt, bondholders said they did not understand the risk they had assumed. They said they felt their money was relatively safe because they owned bonds instead of GM stock. These bonds had been rated B3 prior to their default.

The General Motors bankruptcy is particularly interesting because of the involvement of the US government. Having already loaned GM $13.4 Billion in a rescue package, Congress, and US President Obama backed a plan would have given the United Auto Workers 39% of the company for their $10 Billion in claims, 50% to the government for its $13.4 Billion and just 10% to bondholders, for their $27 Billion in claims. When the bondholders balked at the inequity, Obama called them greedy "money people." Bondholders stood their ground and threatened legal action, and eventually got about 30 cents on the dollar.[1]

The list of companies over the years that have filed for bankruptcy, and left bondholders out in the cold has more than just GM in the way of household names. Chrysler filed in the same year (for the second time), costing creditors $6.9 Billion. Others include R.H. Macy's - $1.4 Billion; Owens Corning - $3.2 Billion; Enron - $10.8 Billion; WorldCom - $30 Billion; Confederation Life - $2.4 Billion. And these were dwarfed by the failures of Lehman Brothers, Washington Mutual, and bailouts of Fannie Mae, Freddy Mac, Bear Sterns, AIG, Bank of America, Citigroup, J.P. Morgan and so may other financial institutions in 2008. Many of these companies boasted the highest credit ratings issued by the major bond-rating agencies.[2]

Canada has not been without its own high-profile bond defaults over the years. Campeau Corporation's $7.0 Billion bankruptcy back in 1990 set a record for its day; broken in 2001, when real estate giant Olympia and York filed for $12.2 Billion, then Air Canada in 2003 for $12.9 Billion. And although shareholders losses got most of the headlines, Nortel bondholders were on the hook for $4.1 Billion when the one-time blue chipper finally filed for bankruptcy in 2009.₃

Investors who ignore the risk of default, not only by corporations who issue bonds but by highly rated financial institutions as well, should reconsider their position, as one day, they too, may be left out in the cold.

There are a myriad of things that cause a stock market to fluctuate up or down; some related to a single issue, most of them which make headline news, and all of them eventually tied into future earnings. Bond markets can be influenced by individual events as well – such as the above list of defaulted securities, but mostly they are influenced by interest rates.

Investors have long recognized that there is an inverse relationship between the value of existing bonds and the interest rate trend. As interest rates go up, bond values go down, and vice versa. This is not just a theory or opinion, but a mathematical certainty.

Let's assume that today I purchased a 3 year Government of Canada bond for $1,000 that will pay me $50 interest in one year, another $50 the following year; and yet another $50, along with the return of my principle three years from today. The market interest rate for three-year bonds today is 5.0%, so my bond is worth $1,000 today – the same as its face value.

Now, suppose tomorrow The Bank of Canada raises short-term rates so high, that three-year bonds now yield 6.0%. But my bond only pays 5.0%. How much less is my bond worth than the new 6.0% bond? To start with, today's bond pays $30 less over the 3 years, so my bond value is close to $30.00 lower because of the interest rate change. In fact, due to the time-value of money (ie: interest on your interest), it is actually $27.75 lower; so my "today's" $1,000 bond is now worth only $973.25.

The truth is that most bonds pay interest twice yearly, but assuming an annual payment makes the math easier to illustrate.

How much impact would this have on a full bond portfolio? Well, let's say you are wary of corporate bankruptcies, and decide that, for safety's sake, you will only invest in Government of Canada Bonds (AKA: Canada's) So, you purchased $10,000 of a 10 year Canada bond at par ($100 for every $100 face value). The interest rate is 4.0%. Now, let's say the market interest rates moved up to 8.0%. (Not possible? - I can remember when they went to around 16% for this type of instrument!) Your $10,000 bond investment is now worth $7,281.90.

That's a 27% loss on the safest investment you could think of! Imagine having a whole portfolio of Canada Bonds and watching the value falling by 27%.

Chart 3.1 illustrates how this powerful inverse relationship has affected bond returns as the interest levels gradually declined over the last 32 years.4

Chart 3.1

Canadian Bonds vs Bank of Canada Rate

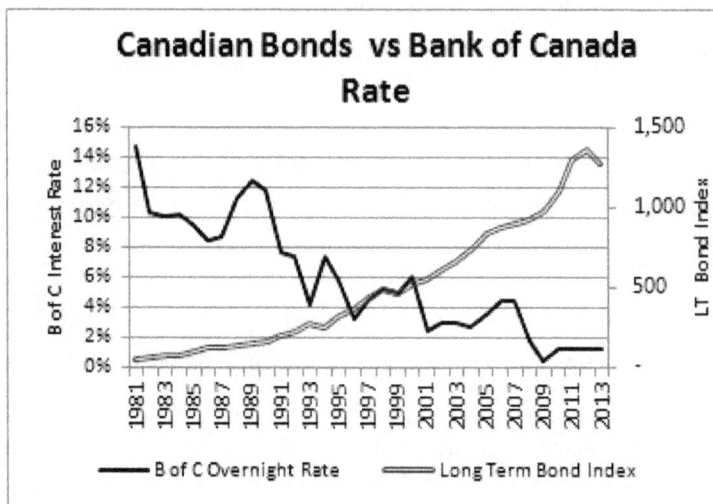

Canadian 90-day T-Bills reached 18.4% in 1981 before they began to fall. By the end of 2013, those same T-Bills sat at just over 1.0%. This resulted in extraordinary bond returns.

The 1970's was a decade of excesses. Oil prices trended in the sub-$20 per barrel range in the early part of the decade, before the first OPEC embargo in 1974, when oil spiked up to the $50 range; ushering in the 1974 recession. The western world seemed to be getting used to the new reality when OPEC struck again in 1979; squeezing supply, and driving the oil price up – this time to $110 per barrel by early 1980. Again, this was a major contributor to a recession. This one was a double-dipper, and the worst recession since the 1930's.

As all this was happening, the infamous "Baby Boom" generation came into adulthood, and demand for everything from cars to stereos (and houses) was at an all-time high. In

26

order to accommodate all this demand, western governments started ratcheting up the supply of money, and when the supply of money increases, so does inflation.

In the US, M2 (a measure of money supply that includes cash and checking deposits (M1) as well as savings deposits and money market mutual funds) had been growing at a rate of about 7.5% annually in the 1960's. This rate increased to the 12.5% range in the early to mid-1970's. In Canada, M2 grew at 10% or less in the '60's; rising to 16% in 1973 – and peaking at 22% in 1974. It then leveled off; staying in the 15%-16% range until 1981.₅

US inflation was tame in the early 1960's; registering about 2.0% until picking up in the latter half of the decade. By 1975 US CPI inflation was 12.5%, and it finally peaked in 1980 at 15.0%.

Canadian inflation as well, stayed about 2.0% in the late 1960's, then spiked to 9% in 1973, and 12% in 1974. It settled into the 7%-8% range for a while, before jumping again – to 9% in 1979, and peaking at 12.9% in 1982.₆

Paul Volker, Chairman of the Federal Reserve Board in the US and Gerald Bouey, Governor of the Bank of Canada had two tools at their disposal to fight this inflation: curtail the money supply, and raise interest rates. M2 growth was cut back to pre-1970's levels. As cited above, short-term interest rates were driven to nearly 20%. Mortgage rates topped out at 22%, and North America plunged into its worst recession since the great depression of the 1930's.

Bondholders were devastated, Long-term Government of Canada bonds hit 17.5%, and bond prices plunged. Bond yields gradually worked their way back down to historical long-term averages by about mid-2007. CPI was close to 2.0%, and 10 year Government of Canada's yielded about 4.5%. Shortly afterward, an international banking crisis, wrought from excessive borrowing, loose lending practices, and massive mortgage defaults rocked western economies and ushered in another brutal recession.

Again, the tools available to central banks were increasing the supply of money, and lowering interest rates. This has pushed rates to their lowest levels (after accounting for inflation) since the Great Depression. The immediate threat from the banking crisis has passed, but rates have been held down in response to a sluggish recovery from the recession.

Over the last half-century, 5-year bond rates have averaged about 2.35% over the rate of inflation. But in recent years, that has changed. In the last 5 years, the rate of inflation has averaged 0.23% higher than 5-year bond rates. In fact, at the end of March 2014, 5-year bonds paid 0.9% less than the inflation rate. That means people who buy 5-year bonds, will have a negative real return if they hold until maturity. This is the same situation for the shorter-term instruments, Treasury Bills. The average 90-day T-Bill rate for the first 6 months of 2014 was 0.97%.[7] With inflation hovering just above 2.0%, T-bill investors are losing more than 1.0% in buying power on an annual basis – and they pay income taxes on the interest!

But the worst has yet to come for bond investors. Remember, the impetus for near-zero interest rates in the US has been the slow, grinding recovery from the recession that followed the banking crisis in 2008. At its worst, GDP declined nearly 5% on an annualized basis. Unemployment topped 10 percent. Consumer confidence was at its lowest level in recent memory, and housing starts were at a virtual standstill.

It has indeed been a long, arduous recovery, but the Federal Reserve (the Fed) has begun to "normalize" monetary policy. It has begun gradually reducing its money supply growth, and the next eventual step will be to increase interest rates.

That said, US rates will not rise appreciably until the Fed is convinced such action will not derail the economy, and that by not bumping them up, it is contributing to inflation. US GDP has been tracking upward since early 2013, except for a temporary blip in Q1, 2014, when the introduction of "Obamacare" took it off course. It has since resumed its growth, as Q2, 2014 GDP growth came in at 4.2%.[8]

Other solid indicators suggest the US economy is finally getting its "mojo" back are: Consumer confidence has returned, unemployment is down, and although new home sales have not approached pre-recession levels, they have been trending upwards.

This does not mean interest rates are headed back to 1981 levels anytime soon. But, with US inflation hovering in the 2.0% range, it's a safe bet that the Fed will take action gradually. The slight increase in late 2015 was just the beginning of a long, slow rise that I expect will take the Fed Funds rate up to the 2-3% range in the next few years.

And, as we just saw, bond returns depend very much on the direction interest rates are moving. I think it's safe to conclude that the 20-year bull market in bonds is over, and investors are better off looking for somewhere else to put their money.

What about Real Estate?

Real Estate investing can be very rewarding if you have the time, knowledge and resources to put into such an undertaking. It can also be very risky, not only if you do not have those resources, but sometimes, even if you do. One only needs to think about the US Real Estate implosion in 2008 to realize this is a market that carries some serious risk. Some might claim that the Canadian market avoided those excesses, and we could never see such a calamity here, but even Canadian real estate can and does occasionally have down markets.

Still, over the years, fortunes have been made investing in real estate, and the sector demands that we give it consideration. There are various ways to participate in this market. A few of them constitute actually investing, and there are those I consider speculating. To invest in any asset is to put money into it with a reasonable expectation of generating profitable returns through income and/or appreciation in value.

To speculate is to engage in a transaction involving considerable risk, on the belief that the asset in question is currently mispriced in the marketplace, or that some extraneous event may occur that will alter the market price, so as to generate a very quick or large profit. If you type "real estate - get rich" into Google, you will find there are no less than 75.8 million websites available to teach you how to "get rich" buying and selling properties. I haven't yet found the time to review all 75.8 million sites, but you can bet that the vast majority of them will encourage you to speculate – not invest – in real estate.

Some of the more speculative strategies in real estate involve "wholesaling", whereby you look for properties for which the asking price is below the actual market value. Once you find your target property, you enter into a contract to purchase it, then immediately put it up for sale at a higher price. The joy of "wholesaling" they say, is that you never actually own the property, and there is no risk. – No risk?

Suppose you got your valuations wrong, and you are unable to sell the property before the closing date? At the very least, you will lose your deposit – which typically would be a few thousand dollars at the minimum. And if you earn a reputation as some-one who fails to close deals, you soon won't be able to find a reputable real estate agent who is willing to even deal with you.

Another speculative practice is known as "flipping" houses. This has gained popularity along with certain reality T-V shows. In this case, you actually buy the property - perhaps renovate it as the T-V shows depict, and hope you can find a buyer who will pay more for it than you did, plus sales/legal fees, mortgage interest, taxes, insurance and your cost of renovations.

Let's consider what may happen if the market turns down. Not like 2009 in the US, when the average house price fell by 23%, but just a nice 10% correction or so. You have bought your "fixer-upper" for $200,000 – hoping to sell it for $250,000 after renovations. You pay up the minimum 5% down payment, so your initial outlay is $10,000. Then you have legal fees of $4,000. Now you spend $20,000 on new plumbing, wiring, kitchen cupboards etc., and you are ready to sell.

But the market has fallen off, and you can't get a decent offer; at least not one that covers your expenses, so you hold off until you have now owned the house for 3 months, and finally sell it for $220,000. You incur legal fees again, at $4,000, real estate commissions of 5%, or $11,000. So far, you have spent $39,000 more than you got back, plus about $2,400 in mortgage interest and, at least, another $1,600 for heat, electricity and taxes.

That makes a $44,000 loss on your original outlay of $10,000 or 440% of your initial outlay. Real estate speculation is not easy, and unless you have an inside track……. like being a contractor, real estate agent or real estate lawyer, my advice is- don't try to get rich speculating in real estate.

For most people, their first foray into the real estate market is the purchase of their own home. Depending on your personal family and cash flow situation, it may be a good investment because you would have to pay rent anyway. This may not always be the case, but for the majority of Canadians, owning their own home makes them feel more secure. And most believe the capital appreciation in their home over the years outstripped any gains they would have made by purchasing stocks or bonds. This, too, may not be true.

Chart 3.2

New Homes Returns

Chart 3.2 compares new home prices between 1982 and 2014 with returns from TSX equities and the Bank of Canada Rate. The average new home in Canada sold for $82,200 in 1982 while in July 2014 it sold for $401,585. I have also charted the New Homes Price Index, kept by Statistics Canada.[9] This number differs from the above because it is adjusted for many of the changes made to new housing over the years such as the average house size, improvements to the building code etc. By either measure, home prices have lagged equity markets – and even treasury bills during this span. If you really want to invest in real estate, you will need to concentrate on income.

Investors who are interested in becoming landlords will have a host of other issues with which to contend. They will need to understand cap rates, and be prepared to replace or repair a roof if necessary. Or, perhaps the furnace or water heater needs to be replaced. You also need to be prepared in the event you get a bad tenant. What about your cash-flow if a tenant doesn't pay their rent? Real estate investors are also subject to interest rate risk. Mortgage rates can, and often do go up by renewal time.

One way to avoid most of the worry, and hassle of the above – and to avoid hefty real estate commissions – is to get exposure to the real estate market by investing in the stock of a real estate company, or in Real Estate Investment Trusts (REIT's). REIT's are equity positions in real estate organizations which are set up as a trust rather than a limited company in order to attract preferential tax treatment.

Payments are made to investors as "cash-flows" rather than dividends and are usually more generous than the average dividend yield. On top of that, the properties are managed by professionals. These securities are much more liquid than direct real estate investing, and transaction costs are minimal.

Gold......... for safety's sake?

If you look on Wikipedia, under the history of money, you will find that stamped metal coins were first used as currency in about 700 BC. I'm going to jump all the way ahead to medieval times, famous for Spanish doubloons, and when jolly old England used gold coins, and a pound sterling was literally one pound of sterling silver. This is known as a bimetallic currency system, and these were the currency of England of the day.

Most countries utilized a bimetallic currency system right up to 1900 when the gold standard was introduced. That was cast aside, however in 1933, as US President Franklin D. Roosevelt outlawed private gold ownership (except for jewelry). The gold standard was re-established by the Bretton Woods agreement in 1946, only to be repealed again in 1971, by then President Richard Nixon.[10] Since that time, virtually all countries have used what is known as "fiat" money.

The use of fiat money is the main reason so many "gold buffs" recommend everyone put much or all of their wealth in gold. In those medieval times, when merchants were paid in gold coins for their wares, the less savory entrepreneurs would engage in a practice known as "clipping" their coins; or shaving a small (hopefully unnoticeable) snippet off every coin. This has the effect of debasing the original coins, but by adding all of the little shavings together, one ends up with a nice little extra nugget from time to time.

Fiat money is not backed by gold, but rather by the "full faith and credit" of the issuing government. It is accepted as money because a government says that it's legal tender, and the public has enough confidence and faith in the money's ability to serve as a storage medium for purchasing power.

The problem comes in when a government decides to give a boost to its economy by printing extra currency – usually at a rate faster than the growth of the overall economy – and like the US has been doing since the last recession. This has the effect of debasing the currency – just like the "coin-shavers" of centuries gone by.

Unfortunately, some countries have gone to such extremes that their currency, and ultimately their economy collapsed. In 1994, following significant economic reforms and political turmoil, the heavily indebted Mexican government was forced to devalue its peso. Foreign investors lost confidence, pushing the peso dramatically lower and forcing Mexican interest rates to nearly 80%; crushing the Mexican economy, and necessitating a bailout by the US.[11]

The Asian crisis of 1997 was also precipitated by significant foreign debt and fast growing, emerging economies. In this instance, the US increased its own interest rate, which attracted foreign investment away from the area, and southeastern currencies fell dramatically.[12]

So, as any government – especially one that oversees an economy the size of the American economy engages in practices likely to put pressure on its currency, the gold bugs take notice. If the central bank increases the supply of money, it is expected that inflation will ensue. That just means the value of the currency will decline in relation to everything else. So to avoid the losses which are likely to result from holding any dollar-based assets, it is better to hold something for which the value will not decline. – an asset which is not dollar-based. (Gold)

Gold can be purchased in many forms. The old standard of buying gold wafers or gold coins, and storing them in a safety-deposit box at the bank is no longer the only way to participate. In fact, it may not be the most efficient way at all. These days you can buy gold mutual funds, gold ETF's or even shares in gold trusts.

In the end, however, gold has not shown itself to be a very profitable long-term investment.

Chart 3.3

Gold vs TSX Total Return

- — Gold Price ═══ TSX Total Return

If a picture is worth a thousand words, then Chart 3.3 must be worth a little over $1,400 because gold averaged $615/oz in 1980, and was at $1,394/oz in June 2014.[13] Thus, $100 invested in gold bullion in 1982 was worth $226.73 in June 2014. On the other hand, The TSX Total Return Index was at 2,770 in 1980 and has grown to 45,523 in June 2014, to turn that $100 investment into $1,643.17.

Perhaps gold can be considered a hedge in times of severe economic strife, but to be successful, you need to know when that strife will hit. And – just before the crisis ends you'd better get out of gold because it tends to move down just as fast as it moves up.

Gold traded in the $700 range for most of 2007, jumping up over $1,000 in 2008, only to fall back down to $700. Then it shot up to over $1,800/oz in 2012 on fears of the collapse of the Euro. In 2013, gold fell from a high of $1,693 early in the year, to $1,195 at year-end. That's a level of volatility I don't consider particularly safe, and longer term, the returns just don't stand up to equities. For any-one who insists on having exposure to gold in their portfolio, I would far rather own shares in a top-quality gold mining company - one with a good balance sheet, a good earnings track record, and one that pays dividends.

In reviewing the merits of each of these asset classes, I can't help but conclude the best investment strategy today, and for the foreseeable future is to focus on equities. Buy stocks when they offer reasonable value, sell holdings from your portfolio only as they become overvalued and if you are unable to find equities that are not over-priced, hold the funds in T-Bills, or other money market instruments until prices become back in line.

This way you will be sure to have some of your portfolio out of the market when it inevitably turns south, and you will have cash to spend on under-valued stocks after the market has been beaten down by panicked "Johnny-come-latelys". More on this in my chapters on market timing!

Chapter 4

Accessing Financial Markets

Whether you decide you want to be invested in domestic equities, bonds, foreign equities, commodities, real estate or any combination of the above, there are several ways to access the markets of your choice. There are mutual funds, hedge funds, exchange traded funds and segregated funds. You may choose to invest directly, using a full-service broker, a discount broker or have some-one else do it on your behalf. This chapter takes you through many of the avenues that are offered to give you access to the markets and points out several advantages and disadvantages for each.

Mutual Funds

They are the best of deals; they are the worst of deals. They are acclaimed for their wisdom; they are derided for their ineptitude. At the risk of causing Charles Dickens to roll over in his grave at my bastardization of perhaps his most famous turn of phrase, allow me to explain.

Modern day mutual funds have come a long way since their humble beginnings in the 1920's. The first open-ended mutual fund (the most common type of fund seen today) in North America was founded in Boston, in 1924.[1] Open-ended funds have no limit on how many shares (units) they can issue. As investors buy into the fund, new units are issued, and when they decide to exit the investment, their shares are not sold, but rather redeemed by the fund managers.

By 1929, there were 19 mutual funds competing for investors' business. Today there are over 7,700 mutual funds in existence, managing in excess of $15 Trillion in assets. Funds have become the vehicle of choice for a boundless number of individual investors.[2]

The fact that this is so, suggests that there must be several compelling advantages to investing in mutual funds, yet there is also substantial evidence that mutual fund investing can be fraught with pitfalls, incompetent managers, and unsavory purveyors. Let's start by looking at some of the many advantages:

Diversification:

A mutual fund is a pool of assets set up in a trust, which is funded by a variety of investors, and comprised of stocks, bonds, treasury bills or other securities, or a combination of these assets; or perhaps even other mutual funds. When you purchase units of a mutual fund, you are automatically diversifying.

And, one of the first rules of investing is to diversify your assets. Who has not heard the phrase "Don't put all your eggs in one basket?" This is an issue we will have a closer look at in a later chapter, but the basic principle is this:

Sarah is thinking of buying stock in one of five different companies. CompA, CompB, CompC, CompD and CompE. They all carry the same dividend yield, and the future looks equally promising for each of the five. Sarah considers simplifying things, and just investing $50,000 in CompA, but instead, she decides to diversify, and invest $10,000 in each. As she had hoped, CompB, CompC, CompD, and CompE all provided a healthy 10% return after one year, but to everyone's surprise, CompA lost 30%.

Because Sarah diversified, she gained $4,000 on her combined investment in CompB, CompC, CompD, and CompE, but lost $3,000 with CompA. Her net gain on her $50,000 portfolio was $1,000. Had she not diversified, and put her entire $50,000 in CompA, Sarah would have lost $15,000. Such are the benefits of diversification.

Can you over-diversify? Yes, you sure can. But that is a matter I will address later. What is important here, is that by utilizing mutual funds, an investor can put a very modest amount of money into the market, and achieve instant diversification. What if Sarah had only had $10,000 to invest, and not $50,000? In this case, it would be wise for her to find a quality mutual fund that focuses on similar types of security, in order to achieve the benefits of diversification.

Divisibility:

Michael has a young family and hasn't yet been able to build up a significant investment portfolio. He recognizes the importance, however of saving for the future, and figures he can put away $500 per month toward building one. Michael feels a conservative stock portfolio would best suit his needs. He has read up on Canadian bank stocks, and believes this would be a great place to start, but he notes the average share price is over $60.00.

Michael can't purchase 8.3 shares of his favorite bank, and even if he could, minimum commissions would make his costs prohibitive. But he can purchase $500 worth of units an equity mutual fund. And if he checks around, he will find that there are several funds that specialize in the Canadian financial sector.

Convenience:

Following up Michael's situation, Michael found a suitable fund and invested $500 in it through the brokerage arm of his bank. He would, however, like to repeat this transaction every month for the foreseeable future. He went on-line, and arranged for a recurring purchase of his favorite mutual fund for $500 on a monthly basis, with the money to be automatically debited from his savings account. Michael is now well on his way to building his nest egg.

Professional Management:

OK, this is one feature that most consider an asset, although I sometimes think it should be on the liability side of the ledger. But let's examine the situation for Aidan; a busy young professional who wants to build his own nest egg, but doesn't have the inclination or the time to spend researching stocks, following up brokerage reports or even closely monitoring his portfolio.

Aidan considered signing on with an independent Portfolio Management (or Investment Counselling) firm, who engage in Discretionary Investment Management. Unfortunately, Aidan discovered that most Investment Counselling firms require a minimum initial commitment of $500,000 or more, and Aidan did not have that much to invest.

Two of Aidan's friends have recommended a particular equity mutual fund, and after a quick review, Aidan found that the fund had been run by the same managers for several years and that during that time, the fund had performed fairly well. Even knowing that past performance is no guarantee of future returns (something fund companies are obliged to tell you), he felt comfortable investing in the same fund as his friends. In this way, Aidan was able to gain access to professional portfolio management.

Dividend Reinvestment:

Henry received a modest inheritance when his uncle passed away last year. He wants to keep this money invested, and see it grow for when he gets older and retires, but he doesn't know what to do with the dividends. Some companies allow their shareholders to re-invest their dividends, rather than take them in cash, but that is certainly not always the case. Virtually all mutual funds have an automatic dividend reinvestment plan available. Henry invested in the fund he liked and signed up for the dividend reinvestment plan, and now he doesn't have to worry about what to do with the dividends.

Automatic Withdrawal Plans:

Alice has saved all her life and is now considering retirement. She has several mutual funds, both in and outside her RRSP's which she now hopes will supplement her pensions. Alice feels she will need about $1,200 per month beyond her pension amounts to live comfortably, so she instructs her advisor to set up her mutual funds on automatic withdrawal for $1,200 monthly in total, allocated amongst her funds. In this way, Alice has ensured she will have adequate cash flow to meet her everyday needs.

With all these wonderful attributes, how can any-one not like mutual funds? Well, the dissenters are many, and they come armed with some pretty convincing arguments.

Performance:

According to the 2013 SPIVA (Standard & Poor's Index Vs. Active) Funds Scorecard, only 44.2% of all Large Cap equity funds in the US were able to match the S&P 500 stock index for the year. At first blush, you might think that is pretty crappy, but the truth is 2013 was a very good year. In 2012, only 20.05% of all funds performed as well as the index over a 3-year period, although 27.3% managed to outperform over 5 years. So this means 72.7% of fund managers failed to even match the overall market average. In 2011, a paltry 16% kept up with the S&P 500, and 84% failed. So much for professional management![3]

Canadian equity fund managers sparkled in 2013, as 66.7% of them managed to match or beat the S&P TSX Total Return Index. Looking beyond 2013, however, the glow emanating from Canadian fund managers begins to fade. Over the last 3 years, just 39.5% of them matched the TSX Composite (meaning 60.5% failed to do so); and over 5 years, only 22.2% of Canadian equity fund managers rewarded their clients with returns equal to, or above the average, and 77.8% failed.[4]

I logged into the mutual fund area of the Globe and Mail's "Globe-Investor" web-site to review these funds a little closer. I found 409 actively managed Canadian equity funds that had a track record of 5 years or more.[5] It turns out that even though the average fund beat the TSX Composite by about 4% in 2013, and their average performance virtually matched the market in 2012 and 2011, they did not do as well in 2010 and 2009, however. In fact they underperformed by about 5.8% over the last 5 years.

Of the 409 funds I reviewed, just 11 funds outperformed the index in all 5 years, while 47 funds underperformed in every one of those 5 years. The best single-year performance was delivered by the Aurion II Equity Class F Fund, which beat the market in 2010 by a whopping 50.4%. Unfortunately, this same fund delivered one of the worst single-year returns in 2009, underperforming the market by 36.5%. The cumulative 5-year return for this fund was 28.4% less than the overall market.

The next best single-year performance was the TD Canadian Value GIF II. This fund returned 38.22% in 2011, beating the market by 46.9%. However, it also lost 39.73% in 2010; a year when the TSX Composite provided a 17.6% return. The fund underperformed the market by 57.3% in 2010, and by 74% over the 5-year period.

So, although some funds may outperform sometimes, most of them under-perform most of the time, and the level of consistency is abhorrent! Take heed of that disclaimer that past returns are no guarantee of future returns.

Fees:

So why is it that mutual fund managers can't exhibit more consistency? Why do they find it so difficult to achieve even market returns? A litany of books have been written about this subject alone, but in the interest of brevity, I will only highlight the most pressing issues.

First on everyone's list of why mutual funds tend to under-perform the market is fees. Mutual fund performance numbers are quoted after the Management Expense Ratio (MER) has been deducted. And, as it should be. The MER includes management fees paid to the fund managers as well as any commissions, accounting, and other expenses, and can range from just over 1% on fixed income funds to well over 3% on many active equity funds or asset allocation funds. The average MER for actively managed equity funds seems to be around 2.5%.

Now, perhaps 2.5% sounds like reasonable compensation to gain professional management, pay commissions, tax accounting and the like. But let's say you invest $10,000 in a typical equity fund and – for their part, the portfolio managers match the market returns year after year. Let's also assume the market returns 8.0% annually over a 20-year span.

Had you received the full 8.0% market average annually, your $10,000 investment would grow to $43,157 in 20 years. But hold on – if the portfolio managers just matched the market every year, and the MER on the fund is 2.5%, you only get 5.5%, (8.0% -2.5%) and your $10,000 grows to just $27,656 over the 20-year period. That's a difference of $15,501. Essentially, the fund managers have taken over a third of your profits!

Clearly, the amount of the MER plays an important role in a mutual funds ability to match or beat the market. Historically, although fund companies have been required to disclose MER information to prospective clients, it was usually found in the fine print on page 72 of that prospectus most people never read. Recent changes in regulations are forcing investment advisors and fund companies to be more forthcoming with their fee structure.

Part of these changes will also result in better disclosure of other fee arrangements of which many investors seem to be unaware. These would include commissions (known as loads) paid by you directly to your broker or advisor and trailer fees which are paid by the fund company to your advisor. While it may be hard to imagine an investor not knowing he/she is paying a front-end load commission (because it is paid as a percentage of your investment at the time you make your purchase), it has not always been made adequately clear to investors that they may be assessed a back-end load commission (which is paid as a percentage of your balance at the time you sell your fund).

As well, investors have often been surprised to find that their mutual funds may be subjected to a "deferred sales charge" should they decide to redeem their fund within a certain time frame after purchasing them. This period is usually 5 years, but I have seen some with 7-year terms. Basically, the deferred sales charge is a penalty for "early" redemption that starts out at a certain percentage, and gradually declines until it reaches zero at the end of the specified term. For instance, it may be 5% if the fund is cashed out in the first year, 4% in the second, 3% in the third, and so on.

Load fees and deferred sales charges are not taken into consideration when fund companies report their rate of return, even though they are costs borne directly by the investor. Trailer fees are commissions paid to your broker by the fund company to encourage you to keep your money invested in the fund and are paid out of your MER, so they are reflected in the published rate of return.

Suitability Issues:

Trailer fees are seen by many as a direct conflict of interest for the investment advisor, or financial planner/mutual fund salesperson. Securities regulators compel these advisors to recommend investments that satisfy their suitability obligations to clients. Dealers and advisors have an obligation to understand the general investment needs and objectives of their client, as well as the attributes and associated risks of the products they are recommending to clients.

Even Canadian Securities Administrators admit the suitability standard is a low one.[6] It simply involves the advisor recommending products that match the general needs of the client, not necessarily the product that is in the client's best interest

The bottom line is that an investment advisor or financial planner does not owe his/her clients a fiduciary duty, (more on this later!) and it is, therefore, easy to imagine that some advisors may recommend a fund that, while it technically may be suitable for an investor, it may not be the best fund for the client, but it does pay the advisor a sizable trailer fee.

Market Restraints:

High or hidden fees are not the only reason mutual funds have trouble keeping up with the market. As markets fluctuate, most investors let their emotions rather than their logic dictate their actions. As markets rise to higher and higher levels, people become more and more excited; and they plow more and more money into their mutual funds.

Fund managers have to put that money into the market, so they keep buying stocks – even if the stock prices have been pushed up beyond their true value. To do otherwise would outrage the funds unit-holders, and may very well violate its prospectus. In effect, the portfolio managers are being forced to buy stocks at the very worst time – the top of the market, when stocks are most expensive.

One thing is certain when a market becomes over-bought; and that is that it will eventually go down. And just like when the rush is on to get money into the market, investors tend to run for the exits after the market has gone south. As people panic, and demand their advisors "sell-sell-sell", portfolio managers are now forced to sell stocks in order to meet the redemptions and at the very time they should be buying; at the bottom of the market, when stocks are the cheapest.

This type of "crowd behavior" is short-term thinking, and it is not only damaging to your portfolio, but it makes it nearly impossible for portfolio managers to match or beat the market in the long-term.

Over-Diversification:

Diversification is a good thing, and I have it listed as one of the advantages of mutual funds. It is possible, however, to over-diversify, and that is a drawback shared by all mutual funds.

In my section on diversification, I discuss the optimal number of stocks a portfolio should hold. I observe that a portfolio of one stock can be pretty volatile (and, therefore, risky) and by adding several different issues to a portfolio, that risk can be greatly reduced. (Never put all your eggs in one basket.) I also note that once you get beyond 20 or 30 issues, it is virtually pointless to diversify any further, as cost and effort is increased, but the risk reduction becomes negligible. You would essentially be over-diversifying.

At the end of 2013, the largest Canadian equity fund that didn't specialize in any specific market segment was the RBC Canadian Equity Fund, which held nearly $5 Billion in assets. At mid-2014, the fund had a one-year rate of return of 19.2%, which put it in the 2nd quartile among Canadian equity funds. For 2013 as a whole, though, it returned 12.6%; just less than the 13.0% returned by the TSX Composite Index, but still in the 4th quartile among Canadian equity funds.[7]

This mediocre performance may be related to over-diversification. At last count, the fund held 111 different securities. Thus, the average holding was about $45 million. Now, $45 million may sound like a lot of money. (I know it is to me!) – but to the RBC Canadian Equity Fund, it represents only 0.9% of this very large portfolio.

Let's say the portfolio manager buys $45 million in shares in XYZ Company, and the stock returns 20% in the first year compared to the 10% return of the overall market that year. Certainly, this purchase was an admirable call. The manager must have done a lot of research, and correctly anticipated the company's fortunes, but consider the impact on the overall portfolio - an extra 10% of less than 1% of the overall fund. That is a 0.09% boost to the return over that of the market. Hardly seems adequate for such a fortuitous action, does it?

Of course, if the manager can duplicate this performance with say, another 55 stocks, then the fund as a whole will likely outperform the market. The problem is finding so many stocks that outperform the market by 100%. It just doesn't happen. If there were enough stocks that provided a 20% return, then the overall market return would be higher too, making continuous significant out-performance highly unlikely.

Too Big:

Why do mutual funds over-diversify? Because they are so big. And bigger is not necessarily better. RBC Canadian Equity Fund's largest holding is Royal Bank. (Does any-one else think this could present a conflict of interest?) The next largest holding is TD Bank, as the fund holds 4.9 million shares of TD.

Let's ponder on what might happen should the fund manager lose confidence in TD, and wants to sell his holdings quickly. Between the Toronto Stock Exchange and the New York exchange, TD trades approximately 3.9 million shares per day. The law of supply and demand tells me that if he/she put the whole 4.9 million on the market at the same time, the price would be driven down dramatically, and fund holders could lose millions.

Taxes:

Another disadvantage of mutual funds is the way capital gains within the fund are taxed. If you buy a mutual fund for $10,000 and sell it later for $15,000, you expect to be assessed capital gains taxes on the $5,000 difference in the year you make the sale. This is no different than selling a stock or a bond or any other asset at a profit.

However, mutual fund managers buy and sell stocks within their fund as a part of their daily management. Hopefully, many of their sales result in capital gains – gains that attract taxes. Who is assessed the tax on these gains? The owners of the fund's units at year-end, when the fund must file its annual tax return. This means that if a fund sold a holding in March, and realized a large capital gain – then you bought the same fund in September, six months later, you are on the hook for capital gains taxes on the sale – and not the individual who owned the fund in March, when the sale was made and who redeemed his units in June.

Under the Carpet:

My final forewarning regarding open-ended mutual funds relates to the insidious practice of merging two or more funds – one with a good track record with one or more funds that have sub-standard performance records. The new fund takes on the track record of the better performing fund while the bad fund records magically disappear. Think this is rare? A story by MoneySense Magazine in February 2011 reported that only 42% of the mutual funds that were around in 1990 still existed at that time. "Most were merged into other mutual funds to erase their poor track records."8

There are many reasons to like mutual funds, but there are many more reasons to dislike them. I think for investors who have very modest amounts to put in the market, but recognize the need to diversify, and for those who are putting away small but regular increments into their investment account to build their wealth, mutual funds are a good place to start. But, for people who have already built some equity in their portfolio, there are just too many negatives to view mutual funds as an attractive alternative.

Exchange Traded Funds:

An Exchange Traded Fund (ETF) differs from an open-ended mutual fund in that it trades on the open market, much like a stock. Like open-ended funds, ETF's hold assets like stocks, bonds, commodities or other assets. Most ETF's are designed to track a given market. For example, the original Canadian ETF was introduced in 1990 to track the performance of the TSE 35 stock index, and later the TSE 100. These funds were known as Toronto Index Participation Shares (TIPS).[9]

The fund managers issued shares and used the money to buy a portfolio of stocks that replicated the index exactly. There was no active management, so fees could be kept to a minimum, and investors are effectively able to diversify just by holding these shares. TIPS became very popular, and the ETF market was born. There are now thousands of ETF's available across the globe, and the dollars invested is in the trillions.

In Toronto alone, along with ETF's that track the overall market, you can now buy Bank Index ETF's, Energy ETF's Dividend ETF's Small Cap ETF's Growth ETF's, Bull/Bear ETF's, Covered Call ETF's and the list goes on. Management expense ratios typically range from 0.10% to 1.0%, much lower than most open-ended mutual funds, but some actively managed US ETF's carry expense ratios as high as 8.0%.

ETF's offer many of the same benefits as open-ended mutual funds such as the ability to diversify for modest portfolios and the ability to make smaller purchases or sales. But they also have several other advantages. These include the ability to trade like a stock. Should you decide to redeem a mutual fund, your order is processed at the end of the day, and the price you receive is the closing value. Of course, if you make your request too late in the day, you get the next day's closing price. With an ETF, if you place your order at 10:00 in the morning, it is processed right away, and you get the price at which it traded at 10:00.

There are tax benefits to holding an ETF over a mutual fund as well. Since there is usually much less portfolio turnover in an ETF, there tends to be much less in the way of capital gains realized within the fund. And the fund never has to sell stocks in order to fund redemptions.

Also, as previously noted, as most ETF's are not actively managed, and therefore, fees tend to be much lower than for open-ended mutual funds.

Unfortunately, ETF's have their drawbacks as well. For instance, because they trade on the market just like a stock, they also attract commissions every time you buy or sell them – just like a stock. Now, that might not matter much to an investor who buys a market ETF and plans to hold it for an extended period of time, but for people who like to try their hand at market timing, or otherwise expect to use ETF's as "trading" vehicles, these costs can add up.

As ETF's have been developed to track certain market

segments such as energy sub-index, financial, and gold index etc., investors are lured away from tracking the overall market, and into a different mix of assets and market timing – usually based on some "expert's" forecast. Study after study has shown that 90% of all market timers under-perform the overall market.

Most financial advisors recommend a dollar cost averaging strategy for investors who are in the saving stage of life. Let's say you are able to put aside $100 per week, and wish to buy stocks with your savings. Using mutual funds you are able to put the $100 into the market right away – each week. Yes, this way, you will be investing when the market is at its highest, but you will also be buying in when it is at its lowest, so it all kind of balances out. Typically this is more successful than trying to time the market. If on the other hand, you are buying ETF's, you won't want to pay the minimum commission (even at a discount broker) every week. So, you save up enough that you are comfortable making your purchase, only to find that the market has risen 12% since your initial savings installment. Do you buy now? Or hold off in hopes the market goes back down? Here we are, trying to time the market again!

Market ETF's can never out-perform the market. If you buy an ETF that holds all the same stocks as the TSX 60 Index ...such as the iShares S&P/TSX 60 (Stock symbol XIU) – each stock with the identical weighting as the index, your return will be that of the index minus a management fee. (In this case, it is currently 0.17%.)

Specialty and actively managed ETF's can be way more volatile, and less productive than the overall market. This could be a result of poor judgment on the part of the managers, but could rather be from a lack of liquidity and a low volume of trading. For instance, the Horizons AlphaPro North American Growth ETF (HAW on the Toronto Stock Exchange) fell 33%, from $12.04 to $8.01 in January 2011 on low volume, just to rebound weeks later. In July of the same year, the fund fell over 20% and recovered it all by February 2012.[10]

Or it can be a result of unfavorable market conditions for the industry the ETF is tracking. For example, the iShares S&P TSX Capped Materials Index ETF (XMA on the Toronto Exchange) peaked at $24.87 in April 2011. Over the next 24 months the fund lost over half its value, and it has traded in the $12 - $15 range ever since. Similarly, the iShares Oil Sands Index ETF peaked in March 2011 at $22.85, and fell to $12.45 in just six months. These shares have also languished in the $12 - $15 range ever since. Of course, this poor performance parallels the market price of the underlying commodities.

Is it possible to over-diversify and under-diversify at the same time? If you hold an ETF which tracks the TSX Composite index, you effectively hold about 260 stocks in your portfolio. Does any-one need to hold 260 stocks? Even most mutual funds draw the line at around half that. If you read my section on diversification you will conclude that a portfolios optimum diversification is achieved with about 20 – 25 stocks.

However, what happens when a market sector trades so high that it becomes a disproportionate fraction of the index. Let's say the energy sector accounts for 25% of the TSX Index, and oil companies have such a good year that all oil company stocks double in price. Let's also assume the rest of the market had no return at all. So, if the energy index had a value of 25 at the beginning, and all others had a value of 75, the whole index would have had a value of 100. But the energy index now has a value of 50, and the rest is still at 75, so the whole index is now at 125, and the overall return was 25%.

But look what has happened to the energy index as a percentage of the overall index. It has gone from 25%, before its big gains (25/100) to 40% now (50/125).[11] Considering the 35% drop in energy stocks during a 6 month stretch in 2011 and the 28% fall (so far) in the latter part of 2014, I would suggest that is not a good idea.

This problem isn't just restricted to a given sector; it could be focused on an individual stock. At its height, Nortel Networks accounted for more than a third of the total valuation of all the companies listed on the Toronto Stock Exchange (TSX).[12] So if you held an ETF that was designed to mirror the TSX, you effectively had one-third of your portfolio in one stock; Nortel.

In September 2000, Nortel stock peaked at $124 per share. Subsequently, Nortel shares fell precipitously, and eventually they became worthless. The company's market capitalization fell from C$398 billion in September 2000 to less than C$5 billion in August 2002. If you held only that ETF that mirrors the TSX, Nortel took along with it, one-third of your portfolio value. Even if you wanted to sell just the Nortel part of your portfolio, you couldn't.

Like open-ended mutual funds, ETF's can offer some tangible benefits; but, also like mutual funds, they have some serious deficiencies.

Segregated Funds:

A segregated (seg) fund is a mutual fund wrapped up with an insurance policy. Seg funds offer many of the same benefits and pitfalls of mutual funds with a few added twists. For example, because they are connected to an insurance policy, they are insulated from creditors, should you ever go bankrupt. As well, so long as you have named a beneficiary, they are exempt from probate fees when you die.

But more noteworthy, is that they come with a redemption guarantee. That is, provided you hold your seg fund for a certain period (usually 10 years), the company guarantees you will receive no less than a certain percentage of your invested capital when you cash out. This is normally 75% or higher. Of course, you must hold the fund for the full 10 years to make use of the guarantee regardless of how well or poorly it performs. And for the record, North American markets have traded at a level below their value of 10 years past only once – ever.

But the companies who issue seg funds charge very high fees - as much as 4% a year, which is significantly more than what most mutual funds charge, and up to 10 times what many ETF's charge. Where does the higher fee ultimately show up? - On your bottom line. That is why seg funds generally provide lower returns than most mutual funds.

Principal Protected Notes:

A Principal Protected Note (PPN) is similar to a seg fund, in that it guarantees your principal will be returned at the end of a certain time frame. Terms range up to 10 years. Typically PPN's are tied to a certain equity market such as the S&P/TSX Composite Index, and they pay investors a percentage of that market returns. Some PPN's pay out up to 75% of the market return, but I have seen somewhere the payout is maxed at as low as 25%.

In addition to sales commissions and early redemption fees, PPNs may charge management fees, performance fees, structuring fees, operating fees, trailer fees, and swap arrangement fees. With these high fees, restrictions on returns and locking in period, I won't be buying a PPN any time soon.

Hedge Funds:

Hedge Funds are generally high risk/high reward investment vehicles. A Hedge Fund is a pool of capital that invests in a variety of different strategies. They are usually structured so that the fund managers can take long and short positions in order to exploit both up and down markets. A transaction for a long position is one whereby the investor buys a stock or bond etc. and pays for it. A short position is one whereby the investor sells an asset he/she doesn't actually own; hoping the market price will go down, and he/she can buy it back later at a lower price. – A risky proposition indeed!

Because of their nature, hedge funds are largely unregulated; and for that reason, their use is restricted to "Accredited Investors". An accredited investor is defined as certain institutions or individuals having among other things, financial assets of more than $1 million or net assets of at least $5 million.[13]

Wrap Accounts and Pooled Funds:

Many investors looking to simplify their financial matters are attracted to wrap accounts. Wrap accounts are considered by many to be the "poor man's discretionary investment account". This is because wrap accounts generally have lower minimum investment amounts, and they don't offer quite as much flexibility as a regular discretionary investment account.

A wrap account is one in which a bank or broker manages an investor's portfolio for a flat annual fee. The investor usually completes a questionnaire and is then offered a portfolio consisting of several pooled funds. A pooled fund is similar to a mutual fund, except that it does not have a prospectus, is specifically designed for certain wrap accounts and is not otherwise available to the general public.

Pooled funds have many of the benefits and drawbacks of mutual funds, including that of over-diversification. And a typical wrap account will hold several pooled funds in order to meet clients' desires for entry into specific markets. So, an investor may hold units of a Canadian equity pool, a US equity pool, and perhaps a North American equity pool. Ultimately, clients end up holding beneficial ownership in shares of hundreds of companies. Quarterly statements often break down this beneficial ownership so clients can see what they really have in their portfolio – right down to fractional shares.

Often, the various pooled funds within a wrap account will hold the same security. So, an investor may look at his/her quarterly statement and find they hold 43.62 shares of General Electric in their US equity pool, and another 26.85 shares of GE in their North American equity pool. Too much diversification! It only takes 20-30 stocks to optimize diversification in a portfolio.

One disadvantage of wrap accounts and pooled funds that mutual funds do not have is that pooled funds are not transferable. That is, if you want to transfer out from your bank/broker, you will have to liquidate the entire group of funds. This can result in some pretty stiff capital gains taxes if you have held them for any length of time.

Discretionary Investment Management:

Discretionary Investment Management is the delegation of the day-to-day management of your investments to a professional Investment Counsellor/Portfolio Manager (IC/PM).

Essentially, Discretionary Investment Management is a continuous process, which entails:

- analyzing a client investor's goals, objectives, and constraints to develop an investment profile for that client;

- studying the investment climate, in order to determine the most suitable asset mix strategy;

- carefully selecting and building a portfolio of securities, designed to meet the client's goals and objectives;

- then monitoring both the market and the investor's profile, and rebalancing the portfolio as needed.

Your Portfolio Manager would typically invest in individual securities (as opposed to mutual funds or pooled funds), directly in the market on your behalf, meaning you directly own each individual security. Dividends are paid directly to you or your account, and you are responsible for capital gains taxes only when a security is sold on your behalf, where a gain was made.

Because the portfolio is constructed for the individual, and not for the masses, there is no need for over-diversification.

As indicated earlier, the suitability standard required of investment advisors and financial planners is a low one that simply involves the advisor recommending products that match the general needs of the client, and not necessarily the product that is in the client's best interest. It falls well short of what is known as fiduciary duty. Individuals licensed as Investment Counselors or Portfolio Managers, who practice discretionary investment management, however, legally owe their clients a fiduciary duty.

A fiduciary duty is a legal duty for a person (in this case, your Portfolio Manager) to act solely in the interest of another party. The IC/PM's owing this duty are called fiduciaries. Fiduciaries may not profit from their relationship with their principals unless they have the principals' express informed consent. They also have a duty to avoid any conflicts of interest between themselves and their principals or between their principals and the fiduciaries' other clients.[14]

While Discretionary Investment Accounts are more flexible and personalized than any of the 'pooled' vehicles, they generally require a much higher minimum investment than the other approaches. Many IC/PM's require a minimum of $500,000 while some set the minimum at $1 million.

Individual Brokerage Accounts:

Not everybody is prepared to hand over their life savings to another person or persons to invest on their behalf, even if that person is a well-respected fiduciary. And it is these investors for which most of this book is written.

At the time of writing, there were 188 Investment Dealers registered with the Investment Industry Regulatory Organization of Canada (IIROC).[15] Each of the major banks has a subsidiary Investment Dealer, as well as a discount brokerage. You can find a list of these dealers at the following web page:

http://www.iiroc.ca/industry/pages/dealers-we-regulate.aspx

While it is not within the scope of this book to analyze the services of each of these firms and recommend one, I will comment briefly on some of the advantages and disadvantages of full-service vs. discount brokerage firms.

The biggest advantage of using a full-service broker is the individual attention you should receive. This will be especially important for novices, who have very little investing experience. Investment Advisors (IA's) are trained to provide professional advice and are required to adhere to a continuous educational programme by the Investment Industry Regulators of Canada (IIROC) to ensure they keep abreast of new developments and regulatory issues. As noted above, IA's are required to follow the suitability rule, although this falls short of fiduciary duty.

Full-service brokerage firms also provide access to their company's research. Many of the larger firms produce comprehensive economic reports, as well as analysis of markets and individual companies. While much of their earnings forecasts may be of questionable value, their review of assets and past performance can be quite useful.

As well, if you want to participate in Initial Public Offerings (IPO's) you are most likely to find dealing with a full-service broker gets you much more access than discount brokers.

On the other hand, if you are a do-it-yourself investor, and you are not looking for advice or handholding, and you are comfortable doing a little research on your own, you may find a better fit with a discount broker. Working with a discount broker can result in substantial savings on fees and commissions.

Where it may cost hundreds of dollars just to sell 300 shares of your favorite bank and another several hundred dollars to buy 300 shares of your favorite utility company by using a full-service broker, you could make the same two trades at a discount broker for just $20.

Many discount brokers provide access to third party research or even comprehensive trading platforms for your computer. MoneySense Magazine[16] provides an excellent review of Canada's best discount brokerages on the following web-site:

http://www.moneysense.ca/invest/canadas-best-discount-brokerages-2014

As well, The Globe and Mail provides a review of Canada's discount brokerage firms on an annual basis.

Once you have decided on which broker best suits your needs, you are ready to start building a portfolio designed to beat the market. Not sure you have what it takes? Keep reading, and I'll show you how.

Chapter 5

Can the Market be Timed?

The Chartist and the Nayer...

This is a question that has divided analysts, financial economists, and market-watchers for generations. There are Nobel Laureates who say it cannot be done because the market is too efficient. There are other Nobel Laureates who say if you can't tell whether the market is over or undervalued, then it is because you are letting your emotions cloud your judgment. The latter group is newer and has evolved into a branch in economics known as behavioral economists.

So, can markets be timed? Well, yes, maybe sometimes – sort of – but not so much. And check your emotions and biases at the door! They lead to short-term thinking. And, invariably, short-term thinking leads to long-term misery.

I will repeat that for you, just in case you missed it: <u>Short-term thinking leads to long-term misery</u>.

Last week I picked up some pecan butter tarts at the farmer's market. Deep in my neo-cortex (the rational part of my brain), I know I should stay as far away from these sap-dripping, calorie laden little pastries as I can. But my limbic system and sensory-cortex (emotional and sensory parts of the brain) are telling me "Go for it!" I went for it – and over the next few days, I ate the entire lot...... and they were so good! (Short-term thinking.)

Next week, when I go for my annual physical, and I step on the scales, I will no doubt pay for that short-term thinking with some longer-term misery.

I recall from my early investment days, an awful lot of brokers used to stand around the Dow Jones Machine (an old news retrieval system) holding their breath, waiting for the weekly money supply figures to be released. If M1 increased more than had been expected, they would run back to their desks and go on a huge buying spree, believing that lower interest rates and better times were surely ahead. Later the same people would wait impatiently, for the US merchandise trade numbers, knowing that too large a deficit spelled trouble, and wanting to be the first to unload their stock positions.

The fact that all these individuals, holding the same beliefs, acted in the same manner, guaranteed that their prophecies would be fulfilled. Since they believed the stock market was going to run up, they bought stocks. And they did so in sufficient numbers to ensure that stock market did go up thereby proving themselves correct. This is short-term thinking at its best.

Usually within a few days things even out, as some other individual indicator is announced; perhaps this time, not as optimistic and it offsets or even over-shadows the positive mood set by the favorable money supply report. I have always thought of technical analysis as a variation of short-term thinking.

What the Heck is Technical Analysis?

Technical analysts or technicians are chartists who don't concern themselves with such mundane things as P/E ratios, Return on Equity, and the like. This is a breed of investor, who (incidentally is sometimes compared to an astrologer), tries to predict future movements in the price of a stock or the level of the market by studying where it has already been.

The premise on which the technician bases his theory is that human behavior is predictable, and we tend to exhibit the same behavior (and make the same mistakes) time and time again. (Remember George Santayana's quote: "Those who cannot remember the past are condemned to repeat it.")

This being the case, the technician believes that (s)he can look at the chart for a given stock or market index, and find a familiar pattern. Once a pattern is identified, and knowing how a stock's price is likely to move given the history of other stocks which have followed that same pattern, the technician is ready to make his prediction. The modern technician has become more than just a chartist, incorporating, trading volumes and money flow in his work as well as.

Some of the trading patterns identified by technical analysts are actually fairly intuitive. Whether intended or not, they are consistent with behavioral economics theory; that investors' decisions are based more on emotions and personal bias than fundamental value. Support and resistance levels fall under that category.

If a given stock traded down to a certain level – say $51.25, then started moving back up for a time, then weakened to

$51.25 again – and repeated this pattern several times, it can be said to have a support level of $51.25.

Chart 5.1: 1

```
57.5
57.0
56.5
56.0
55.5
55.0
54.5
54.0
53.5
53.0
52.5
52.0
51.5
51.0
50.5
50.0
49.5
49.0
48.5
48.0
47.5
```

Notice how the price has a difficult time
falling below the support of $51.25

| | July | August | September | October | Novemb |

Chart by MetaStock

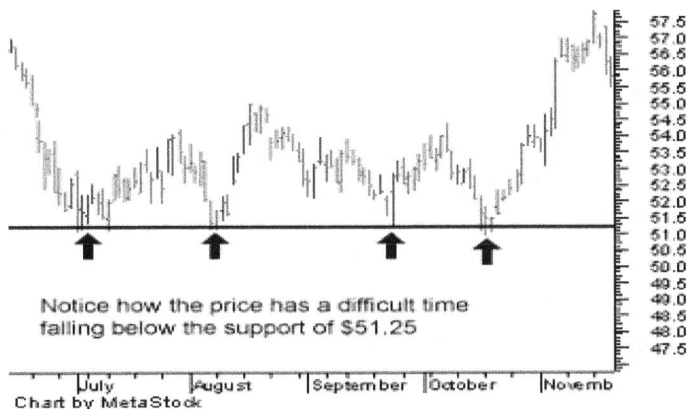

Because investors have seen this pattern repeat itself several times, they expect it to continue. So, as the stock falls toward $51.25, there will be people looking to buy, expecting the price to go back up. It becomes a self-fulfilling prophecy. No consideration is given to future earnings or cash flow potential. No question, this is short-term thinking.

What happens when the company announces its quarterly earnings, just as the stock trades down to $51.25, and the earnings are lower than had been expected. The stock trades below $51.25, and all bets are off! Now it could trade down to $31.25 – who knows? Now that's long-term misery.

Will it really trade down to $31.25? If we depend solely on technical analysis and ignore the company's fundamentals, there is no way of knowing. And that is why I have always had serious misgivings about relying on technical analysis.

Resistance levels work in the same manner as support levels, except that investors are expecting a stock (or the market as a whole) to sell off when it reaches a certain level, just because it has done so before.

Another highly popular tool used by technical analysts is the 200-day moving average. Analysis of moving averages, although based on the principle that markets tend to revert to their mean, still lacks a quantitative comparable. It really just compares the market to where it has been over time, with no justification as to why it trades at those levels. It would be much more meaningful if the market were compared to some measure of value. For example, price to earnings.

Some investors prefer a shorter average a (50 day or 100 day), but the 200 day is by far the most popular. The chart below illustrates the S&P 500 Index (depicted by the blue line) and its 200 day moving average (depicted by the red line).[2]

The 200-day moving average is calculated by totaling the closing value of the index for each of the most recent 200 days, and dividing by 200. At the end of each trading day, the latest closing value is added, and the oldest number is dropped. The strategy is to buy when a stock – or the market itself crosses above the 200-day moving average and to sell when it crosses on the way down. Like support and resistance levels, it is a strategy that works pretty well - except for when it doesn't.

Chart 5.2 ₂

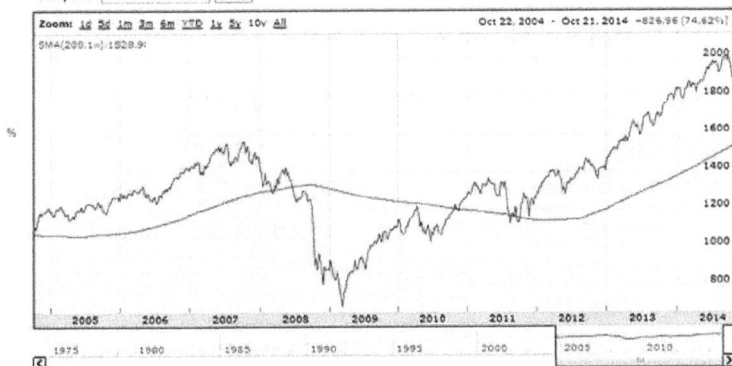

1,936.52 +32.51 (1.71%)
Real-time: 2:14PM EDT
INDEXSP real-time data - Disclaimer

Range 1,909.38 - 1,935.82 &+1 45
52 week 1,737.92 - 2,019.26
Open 1,909.38
Vol 301.33M

Note in March 2008, the strategy would have you selling out at just under 1300, only to have you buy back in less than a week later at the same level. That's a lot of work, and probably commission money gone to waste. But also note in June 2008, it had you selling out at a level just over 1300 and saving you from a 48% free-fall that devastated many investors, and took them out of the market for good.

The problem was that the market virtually doubled, and was just 7% below your sell-out level before the strategy got you back in. After selling out, and buying back in twice in 2011 (at a level below your 2010 buy level), following the 200-day moving average strategy allowed you to garner significant gains.

There are many other patterns technicians use, such as up-flags, down flags, up pennants, down pennants, head and shoulders formations, cup and handle, double tops, double bottoms; and in case these two didn't work out there are triple tops and triple bottoms. I could go on, but I have trouble finding credibility in the practice of drawing funny pictures on stock charts in hopes of determining how I should invest my hard-earned savings.

The Efficient Markets and EMT

Early 20th century economist Irvin Fisher published a work in 1906 called "The Nature of Capital and Income".[3] Fisher was unique in his day because he was also a mathematician, and in his work, he outlined how complex formulae and probability calculations could be used to predict stock prices.

Fisher was spectacularly successful in the market, and by the mid-1920's he had amassed a fortune in stock market profits. However, during that time, his ideas about the market changed, and he came to believe that since the market represented the collective wisdom of all individual investors, and as such, whatever level the market was at, it must be correctly priced. In late 1929, Professor Fisher lost his entire fortune.

Irvin Fisher is likely better known for being completely oblivious to the stock market bubble that ended in the 1929 crash, rather than the historical insights he provided in his earlier work. Unwittingly, he became one of the earliest prominent Efficient Market Theorists.

The Efficient Markets Hypothesis or Efficient Markets Theory (EMT) is a big deal to plenty of professional investors. In fact, two of the most renowned economists who tout this theory recently won Nobel prizes for their efforts. Most people know of it as the Random Walk or Dart Board Theory. The two economists are William Sharpe and Harry Markowitz. Their work inspired Burton Malkhail to write his book A Random Walk Down Wall Street. [4]

> **The strong form** of EMT is based on the belief that the dissemination of information relating to capital markets is so efficient, that securities prices always reflect all public and private information there is to know about a company. Thus, no matter how good you are, or no matter how much research you do, you cannot beat the market. Peter Lynch, John Templeton, and Warren Buffet might not agree.

Exchange Traded FundExchange Traded Fund

The theory is based on the assumptions that the market consists of a large number of profit maximizing participants who act independently of one another, that new information about companies comes into the marketplace in a random fashion, and that no-one has quicker access to it than others. It also assumes that investors are rational and homogeneous, in that they desire the same outcomes from their investments, and that the market price of securities changes instantly, in response to changes in corporate information.

Clearly, however, some investors do have better access to information than others and some are better educated and more knowledgeable in the field of investments; facts that should allow them to extract better returns than some others in the capital markets.

Analysts spend a great deal of their time estimating corporate earnings. While there may be a consensus range, some forecasts are usually higher while others are lower. And when earnings do fall outside the consensus range, the stock price is almost always affected. If everyone had the same information, this would not occur.

Stocks which have low price to earnings ratios have historically outperformed high P/E stocks. If everyone had the same information and expectations, this could not happen, because investors would flock to low P/E stocks instantaneously and the advantage would disappear. Stocks with low price to book value ratios tend to outperform high Price/BV stocks. This too, could not happen if markets were completely efficient. And finally, how is it that corporate insiders have such a tendency to sell at or near the top? Surely they don't have information that is not available to you and me!

Many proponents of the Efficient Markets Theory have recognized these anomalies, which do not support their theory. As a result, two less stringent, but distinguishable groups have emerged.

> **The weak form** of EMT holds that stock prices reflect all available security market information. Therefore past price and volume information has no relation to the future direction of stock prices, so technical analysis provides no benefit to investors.

> **The semi-strong form** of EMT says that security prices already reflect all public information available. This leads them to suggest that fundamental analysis of past financial statements is of no use.

Later work by Eugene Fama,[5] William Sharpe,[6] Merton Miller[7] and others used the Efficient Markets Theory to help formulate "Modern Portfolio Theory" (MPT).

MPT does not reject the concept that some stocks can provide better returns than others. The theory does, however, make the point that generally, there is a risk-return trade-off. That is, the stocks that produce the biggest gains are usually also the most volatile. (Which MPT interprets as the most risky).

MPT also recognizes the benefits of diversification. Generally, when you buy a stock, you really assume two risks.

1. That the stock might go down because the whole market went down - (market risk), and

2. That the stock might go down because of something to do with the company itself, independent of what the market might do - (non-market risk).

If you diversify your holdings - that is hold a great enough number of different stocks, you can effectively eliminate the dangers of non-market risk. That is because one stock going down independently of the market will likely be offset by unexpectedly better performance of some other stock. Different studies have suggested that it takes from 20 to 30 stocks to diversify away non-market risk. Market risk they say, cannot be diversified away.

So, how do Modern Portfolio Theory (MPT) thinkers suggest you maximize your portfolio returns? Essentially, you build your diversified portfolio so as to minimize non-market risk through diversification and match your personal level of risk-tolerance to your desire for a higher return by increasing/decreasing the risk component (both stocks and bonds) of your portfolio and decreasing/increasing the non-risky portion (which is represented by T-Bills).

And if your desire for return exceeds the expected market return, no problem - you just borrow to increase your positions. If you think back to our earlier discussion on real estate, you know that leveraging to invest can end up very badly.

Excessive leveraging led directly to the stock market crash in 1929 and contributed significantly to the crashes in 1987, 2001 and 2008. On an individual basis, the math is simple. If you buy $25,000 worth of a stock, and it goes down 50%, you lose $12,500 (or 50%). If you borrow $25,000 to add to your existing $25,000, then buy $50,000 of the stock; and it goes down 50%, you have lost $25,000 – or 100% of your cash outlay. Don't do it.

MPT effectively advocates a "Buy and Hold" strategy. Stocks, we are told outperform everything else in the long run, and, since no-one can effectively time the market, why not just buy a decent ETF or mutual fund and hold it for ever? Presuming you have a well-diversified portfolio or are in a well-diversified fund, your portfolio will move in lock-step with the stock market. If stocks, in general, were down 5%, you would be down 5%. If stocks were up 10%, you would be up 10%. - And so on. But, are you OK with seeing your portfolio down 53%, like the market was at one point in 2008? – I'm not. And I'm especially not OK with leveraging to make my losses even greater!

Legendary economist John Maynard Keynes[8] once said: "Markets can remain irrational longer than you or I can remain solvent." In uttering this quip, Keynes exposes the most significant flaw in the Efficient Markets Theory, and therefore in Modern Portfolio Theory; and that is the assumption that investors are always rational. It is just not so!

Otherwise, market crashes would not, and could not happen – again, because astute investors (and in an EMT world all investors are equally astute) would sell any stocks that became overpriced instantaneously, eliminating the threat before it could become a threat. Barring war, or some catastrophic natural event like an earthquake that swallows up New York City, the underlying fundamentals that support an economy do not suddenly reverse violently almost overnight. But markets sometimes do. Just as Tulipmania in the early 1600's, the South Sea Bubble a hundred years later and the stock market bubble of the 1920's, people still get caught up in the emotional paradox between greed and fear from being "left out" – or whatever else drives them, and a new bubble begins.

This emotional climate was prevalent during the bubbles mentioned above, as well as the violent markets in 1987, the dot-com bubble of 2000 and the housing bubble and credit crisis of 2008-2009. A particular sector of the market gets "on a roll", rational behavior takes a back seat, crowd behavior takes over, and the market gets pushed well beyond the limits supported by fundaments values. If markets were always rational, as EMT suggests, these events could never take place.

Surely there must be some middle ground between the seemingly arbitrary approach of the chartist and the submissive, almost defeatist notion of the EMT theorist that the market can't be beaten anyway, so you might as well buy the whole thing, then do nothing.

Oddly, it is the very opposite of EMT's assumption of universal rationality that makes markets so difficult to predict in the short run. (Recall Keynes' comment that markets can remain irrational longer than he can remain solvent.) Yet having some idea if the market is over or under-priced by historical standards can help keep you prepared for inevitable bear markets and subsequent recoveries. There is nothing wrong with being cautious in an over-priced market even when the analysts tell you otherwise.

To do that, it is best to re-visit some of the fundamentals favored by market titans like Ben Graham and Warren Buffet. It's a good approach, and it certainly worked for them.

Chapter 6

Using Fundamentals to Time the Market

As I pointed out in our last chapter, if markets are not always rational, then trying to forecast them using economic fundamentals would be very difficult indeed. Still, many analysts look to leading economic indicators to give them guidance as to how the stock market should be priced. Others view the market as a leading indicator for future economic trends. The reasoning is similar to EMT advocates rationale that investors are astute, and know when they should be buying or selling. But is this really true?

Not according to economist Paul Samuelson who wrote in 1966: "Wall Street indexes have predicted 9 of the last 6 recessions."[1]

Chart 6.1

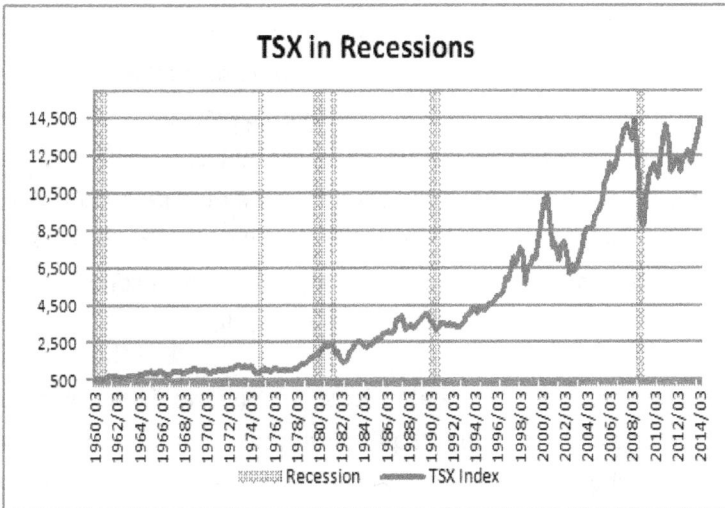

TSX in Recessions

79

On Chart 6-1 we can see the TSX Composite stock index back to 1960, along with the shaded areas depicting Canadian recessions between 1960 and 2014$_2$. It's hard to see on this chart, but the TSX was down about 5.0% in the quarter preceding the 1960 recession. Fluctuations of this magnitude are really minimal, and I doubt any-one would seriously consider it an indicator that a recession was on the horizon.

The 1974 recession, however, was preceded by a drop of about 32% in the six months prior to the onset of the recession. This was just after the first OPEC oil embargo, and market participants correctly viewed that as a potential recession-causing event. Interesting, however, is that the market continued to rise after the 1979 oil crisis, and well into the recession that followed. It finally started to decline after the second leg of the "double-dip" recession took hold; falling over 40% before starting back upwards in 1982.

The market crash of 1987 was not accompanied by a recession, in fact, GDP growth improved in the quarter following the crash in Canada. In late 2000, the dot.com bubble burst, and the TSX lost over 35% of its value. Canadian GDP growth slowed for the next several quarters but remained positive throughout (... although the US suffered a mild recession). And by the time the market began its near-death spiral in 2008 in the wake of the mortgage/banking crisis, the economy had already been in recession for several months.

Upon reviewing this data, it seems nearly impossible to conclude anything other than that not only is it not possible to predict the direction of the market from the level of economic growth, but it is also impossible to predict the economy by watching the stock market.

But, why doesn't it work? Certainly corporate earnings are correlated with economic growth. And it is earnings that ultimately determine stock value. Economists at Bear Sterns didn't see any indication of a housing bubble in 2007. Analysts at Lehman Brothers didn't forecast a financial crisis, and credit rating agencies Moody's, S&P and Fitch reported that most of the outstanding Collateralized Debt Obligations (CDO's) and Mortgage Backed Securities (MBS) were worthy of their esteemed AAA rating. That means each had a 0.12% (one in 850) likelihood of default. In the end, 28% of the AAA rated CDO's defaulted.

During the aftermath of the 2008 market collapse, I came upon a cartoon in one of the financial papers.3 In it, two banker-types (wearing pinstripe suits and carrying fancy attaché cases) were standing at the end of Wall Street, gazing out toward the ocean.

Notwithstanding that Wall Street ends at Upper Bay, and not actually the Atlantic Ocean, a tsunami was developing off on the horizon. As the giant swell grew larger and larger the closer it got to shore, nary a word passed between the two. Still, they stared off towards the water.

The seismic wave finally came crashing ashore with tremendous ferocity, taking out most everything in it's wake. The two bankers were tossed around like rag-dolls, and only came to rest, sitting on their posteriors after the wave had crested and the water was receding. That's when the one banker looked over at the other one and said: "Whoa... didn't see THAT coming!"

I was in stitches. Isn't this exactly the same mindset that took over the world economy and world markets leading up to the financial crisis? Government and consumer debt were spiralling out of control. Mortgage defaults were at all-time highs; the Feds had to bail out several major financial institutions; yet very few economists or analysts thought there was a problem.

Only when Fannie Mae and Freddy Mac (Government sponsored mortgage companies) and the "Big Three" automakers needed bailing out did analysts wake up from their funk. By then, Bear Sterns, AIG, Washington Mutual and Merrill Lynch were on the edge of oblivion.

The author is clearly poking fun at Wall Street analysts who couldn't or refused to see obvious signs that serious trouble was just ahead.

Back in the 1950's and 1960's economists recognized the concept of Rational Expectations and a contrasting idea known as Adaptive Expectations[4]. Rational Expectations suggests investors make choices based on their rational outlook, available information and past experiences. Adaptive Expectations holds that investors place more importance on recent events in predicting future outcomes. For example, if one was forecasting stock market action for the year ahead, and the market had risen in recent years, a person influenced by Adaptive Expectations would forecast the market to increase next year because that is what it did last year.

It seems that in the months (even years) leading up to the 2008 market collapse, the vast majority of economists, analysts and investors were heavily influenced by Adaptive Expectations.

But, not every-one ignored those ominous signs. In late 2004 I wrote a report entitled "The Good, the Bad and the Ugly"[5] in which I described the "Good" – housing starts and retail sales were strong, consumer confidence was high; as well as the "Bad" – Employment growth was slowing, the Balance of Payments was in decline; and the "Ugly" – the Consumer Debt/Service ratio was at an all-time high, and the U.S. Federal Deficit was set to hit "half a trillion dollars".

I commented "Something's gotta give ... To ignore these imbalances and just let the debt pile up could eventually result in a complete loss of confidence in, and collapse of the USD, unheard of inflation levels in the US, and potentially economic depression." - Yet very few people noticed.

In 2005, Paul Krugman of Princeton University[6] and Peter Schiff of Eastern Pacific Capital[7] both expressed concern that there was a housing bubble which could end badly. But most economists and analysts seemed oblivious to the facts – even after the bubble began to burst.

The average mortgage loan/value ratio increased from (an already high) 90% in 2003 to over 100% in 2007. Mortgages 90 days or more in arrears trended around 1.7% between 1979 and 2006. They ballooned to 4.5% in 2007. There were 650,000 mortgage foreclosures in the first half of 2007 I the US. In the first half of 2008, there were 1.2 million, and personal bankruptcies, which increased 33%in 2007, jumped another

32% in 2008.[8] And STILL very few people took heed.

The financial crisis and accompanying "great recession" took most analysts and economists by surprise! In spite of correctly identifying the dot-com bubble in 1996,[9] the man who coined the phrase "irrational exuberance" missed the Real Estate bubble entirely. In his testimony to Congress following the crash, then Federal Reserve Chairman Alan Greenspan admitted: "I never saw it coming." He later penned an article in "Foreign Affairs" in which he made the following statement[10]:

"In the run-up to the crisis, the Federal Reserve Board's sophisticated forecasting system did not foresee the major risks to the global economy. Nor did the model developed by the International Monetary Fund, which concluded as late as the spring of 2007 that "global economic risks [had] declined" since September 2006 and that "the overall U.S. economy is holding up well . . . [and] the signs elsewhere are very encouraging." On September 12, 2008, just three days before the crisis began, J.P. Morgan, arguably the United States' premier financial institution, projected that the U.S. GDP growth rate would accelerate during the first half of 2009."

Since retiring from the Fed, Dr. Greenspan has written a book entitled "The Map and the Territory" in which he attempts to explain just how the overwhelming majority of economists missed so many obvious signals[11]. He pointed his finger directly at an element identified during the Great Depression by John Maynard Keynes, and long since discarded, which Keynes called "animal spirits"[12].

In his 1936 classic *"The General Theory of Employment, Interest and Money,"* Keynes described "animal spirits as: "... the instability due to the characteristic of human nature that a large proportion of our positive activities depend on spontaneous optimism rather than mathematical expectations, whether moral or hedonistic or economic."

It seems Dr. Greenspan has joined the ranks of the behavioral economists, and figured out the root cause of irrational exuberance. Behavioral economics tries to explain why market participants make investment decisions which are contrary to what we normally think of as rational expectations. These are errors in judgment such as over or under-reactions to economic data or other information that would normally cause a rational thinker to take – or avoid taking action.

This behavior may be related to personal biases; for example, one may just prefer to invest in bonds over stocks. It may be the investor had good results in the past, and doesn't want to risk changing his/her paradigms, or perhaps there has been some other influence. Whatever the reason he/she has a personal bias toward bonds.

It is also human nature that we never want to be the recipient of bad news. Likewise, no one wants to be the bearer of bad tidings. So if one or two economic indicators start to point toward an economic or market reversal, it may just be easier to start paying less attention to those particular indicators. After all, some other indicators still remain positive!

I believe the most serious impediment to rational investment thinking is the fear of not following the crowd. It takes a lot of gumption to stand alone in your convictions when every-one around you says you are wrong. I mentioned above, that one of the few economists who forecasted the 2007 housing bubble was Peter Schiff. Mr. Schiff took part in a debate on CNBC in 2006 during which he made his case for predicting a financial crisis. The three other analysts on the show mocked and ridiculed him for twenty minutes as he stood his ground clearly demonstrating how difficult it is going against the crowd.

So, it seems that even if we may be able to use fundamentals, and economic indicators to help us identify when the markets are under or over-valued, there are too many flaws in analysts' interpretation of data that not only make the timing very difficult but very likely exacerbate the damage.

The most significant impediment to realizing positive investment returns is our emotions. I will reinforce this over and over again. It is difficult not to "follow the herd". Analysts will tell you "Buy, buy, buy." when the fundamentals say "Sell, sell, sell." The financial press loves to make big splashy headlines about "disappointing earnings numbers" or "record high retail sales" etc. It sells newspapers. But it is also short-term thinking. It is not seeing the forest for the trees.

Still, I like to have a reasonable, unbiased idea if the market as a whole is under or over-valued. It is useful to keep an eye on the indicators mentioned above. We just can't use them to "draw a line in the sand". Don't get too caught up in the level or direction of any one indicator at any given time. Much more important, in my opinion, is the overall trend of all indicators. That is when all indicators are pointing north, then good. When one indicator of the myriad of them released every month is lower than expected, make a note of it. But don't fall for all the hype generated by the press. Watch for the trends. If several indicators turn soft… or become negative, then start being cautious. Don't sell out.

The flip side of this advice is just as important. When all indicators point south, and a few start to improve, watch for the trend. When several indicators start turning more positive, you should expect to see the market turning up, too. Analysts, economists, and the financial press are rarely ahead of the curve. They are afraid of being wrong and afraid of "going against the crowd". Remember Warren Buffet's advice: "When every-one else is greedy, be fearful. When every-one else is fearful, be greedy."[13]

Buffet's quote certainly sounds contrarian, and I suppose it is, but more importantly, it reflects the conviction that capital markets always revert to the mean. When markets are trading way above their intrinsic value based on historical data, people seem to want to "get in on the party". And the same people are usually "clamoring for the exits" after the market has fallen well below historic values.

Intrinsic value for an investment can be defined as the actual value of all its assets minus any liabilities, or as the present value of its future cash flows.[14] I will take you through an in-depth review of these concepts in the pages ahead.

Analysts and investors alike have been looking for a sure-fire tool for timing the market for 400 years, and for the most part, it has been in vain. Evidence tells us that precise turning points are virtually impossible to pin down. Yet, using the tools I described earlier can help; and may be useful in avoiding extremely over-valued markets.

I have already made reference to missing the forest for the trees. Let's put that analogy to work by determining just what a market is:

1. A medium that allows buyers and sellers of <u>a specific good or service</u> to interact in order to facilitate an exchange. The price that individuals pay during the transaction may be determined by a number of factors, but price is often determined by the forces of supply and demand.

2. The general market where securities are traded.

3. People with the desire and ability to buy a <u>specific product or service</u>.[15]

So a market (say, the S&P 500 or the TSX) is a compilation of all the different securities that are traded as a part of that market. And each of these securities should be valued (mostly) on its own individual merits. For example, the value of Apple Computers shouldn't have much impact on the price of Walt Disney shares other than, perhaps as an alternative investment. Yet because shareholders of Disney may become pessimistic, they could negatively impact market sentiment, and thereby influence the market price of Apple.

And this is where the rubber hits the road! It is for this very reason investors should pay a lot more attention to the individual securities in their portfolio, and less to the rhetoric being trumpeted by the talking heads in the financial media. If you have a portfolio of well-chosen securities and follow a disciplined approach; not only for what to buy but also for when to buy and when to sell them, the trials and tribulations of the overall market should have much less impact on your portfolio.

First you establish the standards by which each of your stocks is measured. Try to define a reasonable valuation for each security you consider buying (using the metrics I describe below). Some investors like stocks with high earnings growth, other measures of price volatility or momentum. Most successful investors utilize certain fundamental measures of value. I have had success focusing on three in particular…. Dividend yield, Price/Earnings and Price/Book Value. I consider these three metrics so important, I have devoted an entire chapter to each.

The trick to minimizing the impact of market gyrations is to define a target range for each of these metrics for each stock and stick to it. Let's say you target a dividend range of 2.0% to 4.0% for your favorite stock. You own 1,000 shares because you bought them when the market was soft, and the shares traded down to the point that the yield went above 4.0%. At the same time, it also met your Price/Earnings (P/E) and your Price/Book Value (P/BV) standards.

But now, the market has traded up so much – pulling your stock with it, that your stock now only yields 1.9%. This is because the price has risen significantly faster than the dividend has increased. Chances are it no longer meets your P/E or P/BV standards as well. Now for the difficult part. You sell the stock. You still like the company, but the stock has become too expensive to meet your guidelines. Don't worry – you will be able to buy it back cheaper at a later date.

Now the task is to find a replacement stock that does meet your guidelines. And here it gets more difficult. Because the market has gotten so high you may no longer be able to find a replacement stock that is priced low enough to meet your standards, and you are left lamenting the loss of one of your favorite stocks. But, take heed...... it's OK! Your disciplined approach to investing is actually doing your market timing for you.

Keep the money you have pulled out of stocks that became priced too high in a bank certificate, treasury bill or Money Market Fund. Eventually, prices will come back down, and you can buy back your favorite stocks at cheaper prices. You will have the cash available because you stayed disciplined. That is why you should never get emotionally attached to any stock. It is hard to sell out, and sit with your money in cash when all your friends – and those talking heads are bragging about all the money they are making in the market. But, if you stick to your plan, it will be you in the end who has made the real profits - and not the emotional investor who buys into the market after it has generated major profits for some investors, and sells in fear after the market has fallen off and now represents better value.

Chapter 7

Diversify, Diversify, Diversify

... but don't over-diversify

It fascinates me when I hear some-one who has recently had a good night at the horse races or has managed to beat the house at the local casino. Some will go on and on about how they won $800 last week, $500 the week before and $625 last month! But you will never - <u>ever</u> - hear about the thousands they have lost in between. A lot of stock pickers are like that. Especially the pro's.

I think it's human nature to want to share with people stories of our good fortune, and even to chalk it up to skill. But when it comes to talking about our not so successful endeavours, well - we don't really want to. It may make us feel/look like a failure.

But let me make this as clear as possible: If some-one (especially an Investment Advisor) tells you they have never made a poor investment, they are either: 1) brand spanking new at the investment game or: 2) they are lying to you.

As a rookie stock- broker in the early 1980's, I was told by one of our research directors that over time, if 60% of an advisor's stock picks work out well, he should be considered successful. I am happy to report that the vast majority of my investment choices have produced positive returns, but let there be no doubt, I have bought stock in a few companies that have turned out to be real lemons. Every investor has.

In fact, Peter Lynch, famous author of _One up on Wall Street_ once said "There's no shame in losing money on a stock. Everybody does it."[1] Warren Buffett, (The Oracle of Omaha) lost hundreds of millions of dollars investing in Bank of America stock, and even more on his airline stocks.[2] Of course, on his way to becoming one of the world's richest men, Buffett made a lot of very good investments, too.

The point of this discussion is that if, in spite of thoroughly researching each company you invest in, one or two of them are still going to go into the dumper on you, then you need to diversify – Don't put all your eggs in one basket.

Let's look at an example and see why. Assume you have a stock portfolio worth $60,000 which consists of three stocks. Each holding is worth $20,000. Two of your stocks provide you with a tidy little return of 12% in the first year. The other, however, ran into serious problems and was down 50% before you could blink. Now you have two stock holdings worth $22,500 each and another which is now worth $10,000. Your portfolio is worth $54,800. You are down a little money, but consider yourself lucky you didn't put all your funds in the stock that tanked.

What if, instead of limiting yourself to three stocks, you bought ten holdings at $6,000 each. Again, all of your stocks except the one were up 12% after the first year. The same loser is still down its 50%.

92

Here's what you have at the end of the year:

nine stock holdings worth:

Their original value of $6,000 plus 12% (or $720)	= $ 6,720
times nine	= $60,480
plus the new value of the 10th stock	= $ 3,000
	$63,480

So, by diversifying, you have reduced your risk, and still have a positive return even though one of your holdings went into the dumper.

Experts say there are two categories of risk; security-specific (or non-market) risk, which we were able to reduce significantly in our last example, as well as market risk. There is an old saying that the tide raises and lowers all boats. They use this analogy to declare that a rising stock market takes all stocks with it and conversely, a declining market takes all stocks down. This is known as market risk, and conventional wisdom (as well as Modern Portfolio Theory) says market risk cannot be diversified away. (Modern Portfolio Theorists should read my last chapter!) On the other hand, security-specific risk is just like the name implies; and that is it is risk related to one specific stock or security, and it can be reduced (diversified away) in the above manner.

So pervasive are the benefits of diversifying, that some pundits think you should have hundreds of stocks...... better yet – load up on handfuls of mutual funds. Or, you could essentially purchase the whole market using Exchange traded funds (ETF's), those baskets of stocks that mimic the market itself. But, WAIT! It is not necessary to buy the whole market to reduce risk by diversifying.

It only takes 10 to 20 stocks to significantly reduce security-specific risk, and 20-30 stocks to build a truly efficient portfolio:

Chart 7.1

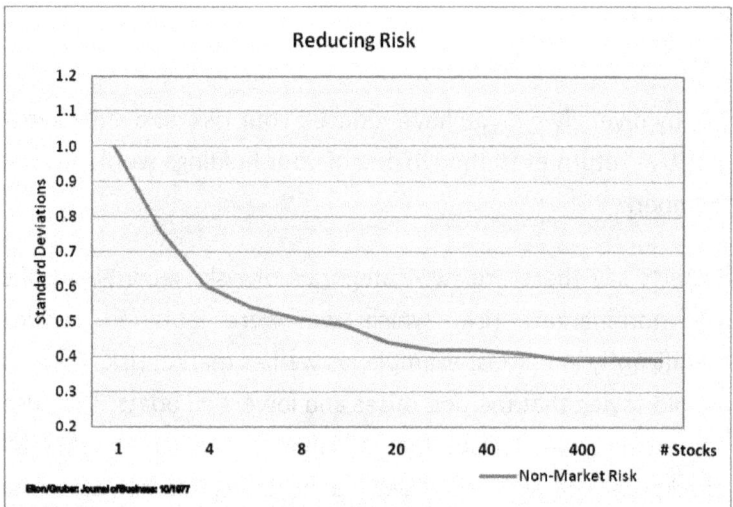

Chart 7.1 was derived from a study done by Professors Edwin Elton and Martin Gruber of New York University in 1977.[3] Elton and Gruber compared the standard deviation of the overall market with a series of portfolios, starting with a one-stock portfolio, then a two-stock portfolio, and kept adding one stock at a time until they had literally hundreds of hypothetical portfolios. On the vertical axis, standard deviation is a measure of volatility for each portfolio, when compared to the overall

market.

What this chart shows is that when you have only one or two stocks, you can reduce non-market risk dramatically, just by adding another stock or two. By the time you have ten or more stocks, the benefit is still noticeable, but less dramatic. And by the time a portfolio has twenty to thirty stocks, you have practically eliminated security-specific risk in your portfolio.

And, that's a good thing, because who has time to study and monitor a portfolio consisting of hundreds of stocks?

Diversification by Asset Class:

Conventional wisdom dictates that you should diversify among asset classes. A quick review of this chart provides a good look at why the consensus feels this way. The three asset classes most commonly referred to by investment-types are stocks, bonds and treasury bills.

Chart 7.2

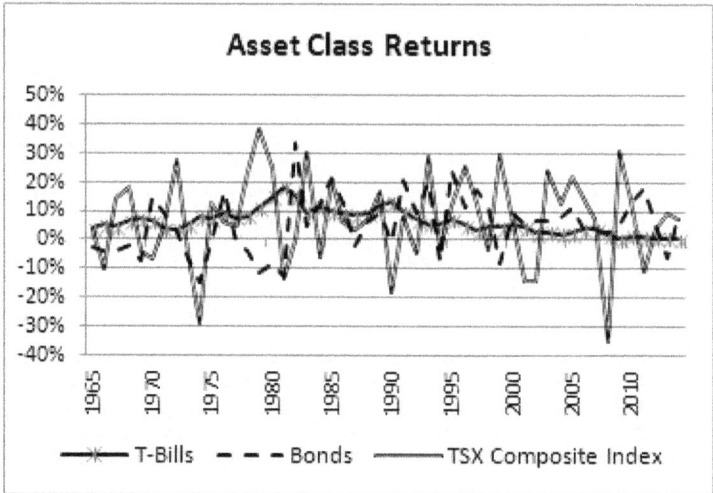

Asset Class Returns

Legend: T-Bills — — Bonds — TSX Composite Index

This chart illustrates the annual returns realized for Canadian stocks, bonds and treasury bills over the 50-year period ending December 31, 2014.[4] At first glance, we notice that there are many periods when bonds are rewarding investors with positive returns while stocks are losing money. And alternately, there are periods when stocks are producing some very lofty returns while bonds are either muddling along or in the red.

What we are to assume from this, is that if we hold a combination at all times of both stocks and bonds; with a little dose of treasury bills rolled in, we can appreciably offset the bad stock years, and have a safer portfolio. The more cautious and conservative you are, the more bonds and treasury bills you would hold, and your portfolio will end up being much less volatile. Except, when you check out the statistical analysis of this theory, we find the argument far less compelling to that which is being sold.

As a statistical measure, correlation measures the relationship between two variables (say the TSX returns and bond returns). If the two variables are "perfectly positively related" they will have a covariance of 1.0 - which really means their performance is identical. Think of it as 100% related. If stocks go up 12%, bonds will go up 12%. If bonds go down 8%, stocks go down 8%. If this relationship existed, there would be absolutely nothing to gain by diversifying between stocks and bonds.

At the other extreme, correlation could be as low as -1.0, which means the variables are "perfectly negatively correlated", and when one variable goes up 8%, the other always goes down 8% etc. If this were the case, holding 50% of your portfolio in each asset would result in zero returns above market – always! In order to make any money above market returns, if this were the case, you would have to switch from stocks to bonds when conditions favoured bonds, and back from bonds to stocks when the reverse was true.

Right in the middle is a correlation of 0.0, which means – you guessed it - zero correlation between the two asset returns. It turns out the correlation between the TSX index over the last 50 years and long-term bonds is 0.09 and the correlation between the TSX and 91-day treasury bills is -0.01; both pretty close to zero correlation. The only way to really gain when this is the case would be:

a.   If one of the assets is both more volatile, yet offers better overall returns (stocks) and you hold a blend of the two assets, based on how cautious and conservative you are. This pretty much guarantees lower overall volatility and lower overall returns. It is also the strategy advocated by most "experts".

b. If you have some insight as to when conditions favour stocks over bonds, and when they favour bonds over stocks; then investing in the asset more likely to provide better returns. As you will come to see, this is the strategy I favour.

In the last 50 years, cumulative returns for these assets are as follows:

Table 7-a

50 Year Cumulative Returns:[5]

TSX Total Return	$7,084
Long-term Bonds	$1,220
91 day T-Bills	$ 2,052

Chart 7.2 tells us that although stock returns can be volatile, but so too, can bond returns. Table 7-a shows us that in spite of the unusually high returns bonds have provided in recent years, over the longer term, stocks have returned nearly six times that of bonds[5].

In my chapter on asset mix, I put forth some compelling arguments supporting a strategy of focusing primarily on stocks, while using T-Bills as a temporary parking spot for your funds when conditions dictate. As a professional Portfolio Manager, by sticking with that strategy and adding some diversification to my portfolios, I was able to exceed market returns over the years. But just splitting your portfolio between 20 or so stocks is not the last word on diversification.

At different stages of a business cycle, financial stocks may be more attractive than say, commodity stocks; or utility stocks may offer more upside than telecoms. As well, there will be periods when US stocks are more likely to outperform Canadian issues or International stocks. This calls for some diversification among industry sectors as well as by geography, too.

Diversification by Industry Sector:

There are 10 different Industry Sectors represented within the TSX Composite Index. The four largest; Financials, Materials, Energy and Industrials represent 77% of the overall index, with another 6 making up the other 23%. Here is the actual break-down as of December 31, 2014:[6]

Table 7-b

Financials	35.74%
Energy	21.96%
Materials	10.61%
Industrials	8.70%
Consumer Discretionary	6.40%
Telecommunications	4.87%
Consumer Staples	3.69%
Health Care	3.54%
Information Technology	2.31%
Utilities	2.18%
TSX Composite	100.0%

It's easy to see how performance has varied among these individual sectors by tracking the iShares ETF that tracks each one. Chart 7-3 chart shows how each of the Financials, Energy and Materials have fared over the last 10 years.7 It was my intent to include the top four in order to cover that 77% of the overall index, but the Industrials ETF only began in 2005.

Chart 7.3

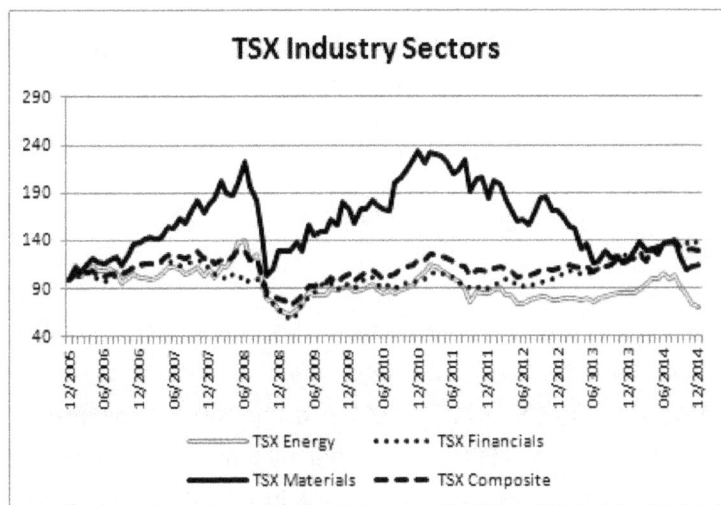

TSX Industry Sectors

The correlation between the TSX and the Financials index is 0.94; between the TSX and the Energy index, 0.66; between the TSX and the Materials index it is -0.33 and the correlation between the TSX and the Industrials index is 0.90.

What we see from this is that if you put all your money in energy stocks, you would have experienced more volatility than the TSX, and ended up with a smaller return. Investing only in materials would have taken you for a wild ride, and you still would have underperformed the overall index. Not surprisingly, Financials, the sector with the highest representation of all had the closest correlation to the overall TSX Composite, and its overall return was slightly higher but very similar to the overall index. Bottom line is that if an entire portfolio of stocks is allocated to one sector, the benefits of diversification (mitigating risk) is wasted.

For example, if you bought 20 stocks in the materials sector in early 2008, the results would have been disastrous, as that sector dropped some 43% between June 2008 and April 2009. By the same token, you wouldn't want to ignore the sector altogether. It finally surpassed its old high in December 2010, after a gain of 83%, which you would have missed if you had no representation at all. And to underline the point, it proceeded to fall 54% by the end of 2014.

Examples of excessive volatility for an entire sector abound. Think back to the real-estate, and home-building sector collapse in the US in 2006-2007; and the ensuing collapse for US financials in 2008. And more recently, the agonizing condition of the energy sector that just kept getting worse throughout 2014. Just as you mitigate individual security risk by diversifying among a sufficient number of stocks, you need to diversify among industry sectors.

Diversify Geographically:

Canadian markets represent about 5% of global stocks by capitalization. The US has about 42%, and the rest of the world accounts for the remaining 53%.[8] Yet many Canadians limit their investment portfolios to Canadian assets. Does this make sense? Well, an argument could be made if the TSX was the least volatile and produced better returns than all other area indices, but a quick look at the following chart tells us this isn't true:

Chart 7.4

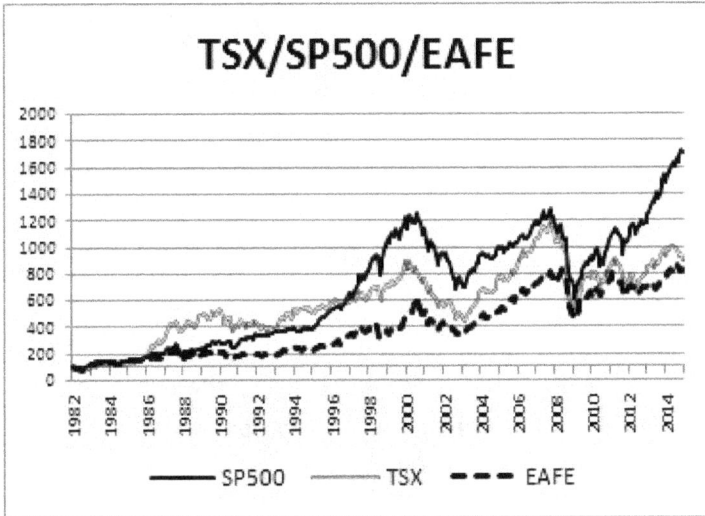

TSX/SP500/EAFE

The TSX Composite Index, of course, is Canada's largest stock index and the S&P 500 best represents US stocks. The EAFE Index (Europe, Asia and the Far East) is a global index that was introduced in 1970 by Morgan Stanley to measure the performance of equity markets in developed countries outside Canada and the US, and is the oldest and most widely used global equity index.[9]

Since 1982, a $100 investment in the TSX Composite Index would have grown to $901 by the end of 2014. The EAFE Index would have grown to $819, and the same investment in the S&P 500 would now be worth $1,710. The correlation between the TSX and both of the two other indices is nearly 0.90, indicating usually that when one goes up, the others do, too. But clearly, there are significant gains to be made investing beyond the Canadian border.

How to Get International Exposure

Most European countries have their own stock exchanges, as do Japan, China and other Far Eastern countries, as well as countries in Central and South America. There are often inherent risks, however, to investing directly in many international markets.

For example, it may be difficult to avoid country-specific risks, be they the risk of economic disaster similar to that experienced by several Pacific Rim countries in 1996, Mexico in 1992 and several other Latin American countries before them, or political risk posed by potential expropriation of assets or a foreign government suddenly imposing restrictions on currency exchange.

Investing directly in many foreign markets can be expensive, cumbersome and risky. Reliable information is not always available for companies in many jurisdictions, and this strategy can also lead to foreign exchange risk. It is also not enough just to allot a certain portion of one's portfolio to "Global" mutual funds, as these tend to under-perform, and to charge excessive fees for doing so. Exchange Traded Funds may provide access to a particular market, but they don't really mitigate political or other country-specific risks. And since they mimic the market, they can hardly be expected to outperform it.

Yet, you can still invest internationally without taking on undue risk related to specific countries by buying stock in multi-national companies. In the US for instance, General Electric earns 53% of its revenue internationally[10]; Exxon – 73%[11]. In recent years, Canada has lost several international companies through take-over. Inco was taken over by Vale CRVD of Brazil.

Alcan was taken over by Rio Tinto of Australia. Yet many Canadian-domiciled companies still operate internationally. Suncor earns 60% of its profits outside of North America[12]; Magna International gets 52% of its revenue from overseas, and Potash 42%.[13]

But there are also many excellent international companies headquartered overseas that Canadian investors have access to. Total Petroleum of France makes 77% of its sales internationally[14]; Toyota is at 61%[15]. Honda, 78%[16]. Anheuser-Bush gets 89% of its revenues internationally[17]; Canon 80%[18], Sony 75%[19] and Unilever 60%[20]. The list goes on.

The giant multinational corporation is hardly a new phenomenon. Nations have been trading goods and services for centuries, and many large companies have inter-listed for generations. In recent years, however, this practice has begun to proliferate at a more rapid pace as trade and other business barriers come down, and companies strive for a bigger share of the world market in search of more profits.

The more successful of these companies will make their shares available to a larger public in order to gain access to more capital. They do this by listing on major North American stock markets (either directly, or by getting sponsored as American Depository Receipts (ADR's). These are the companies upon which we need to build our global investment strategy. Carefully chosen, these are the companies that will provide superior returns for the least amount of risk.

An ADR is like a stock that trades in the United States but represents a specified number of shares in a foreign corporation. ADR's are bought and sold on American markets just like regular stocks and are issued/sponsored in the U.S. by a bank or brokerage firm. The U.S. bank purchases a bulk lot of shares from the company, bundles the shares into groups and reissues them on either the New York Stock Exchange (NYSE), American Stock Exchange (AMEX) or the NASDAQ. In return, the foreign company must provide detailed financial information to the sponsor bank.

The advantages of ADR's are twofold. For investors, ADR's are an easy and cost-effective way to buy shares in a foreign company. They save money by reducing administration costs such as foreign stock exchange fees and other handling charges and avoiding foreign taxes on each transaction. At last count, there are 288 ADR's listed on the US stock exchanges[21]. Given this exposure to the US investor, companies who have their shares listed as ADR's also make sure financial information is accessible and listed ADR's must translate those statements into US GAAP.

When you consider the added risks and costs of investing directly on many international stock exchanges, as well as the high costs of mutual funds and inflexibility of ETF's the best way to access most international markets is by investing either directly in inter-listed companies who list on a US or Canadian stock exchange, or in companies whose shares are available as American Depository Receipts.

Chapter 8

Dividends Matter

Back when I was a graduate student, studying Finance at university, I came across what a couple of Nobel Prize winning economists named Franco Modigliani and Merton Miller termed the "_Dividend Irrelevance Theory_"[1]. Basically they put together a long mathematical argument that claimed that neither the price of firm's stock nor its cost of capital are affected by its dividend policy. In other words, investors should not care whether a company pays dividends or not. Well, I'm not drinking out of that punch bowl!

Modigliani and Miller acknowledged their theory works only if we ignore taxes and transaction costs. Then, if a stock-holder wanted to have an income stream from his/her portfolio, all (s)he has to do is sell a small portion of stock on a regular basis. Since the company is always re-investing its profits, the stock value will rise by the same amount as the "non-dividend", so the investor is in the same position as if (s)he had received a dividend instead.

I'm not sure about Modigliani and Miller, but in my world, I pay both transaction fees and taxes. If I had to sell $250 worth of stock in lieu of getting a $250 dividend; and paid $25.00 in commission, then somebody who isn't me is getting 10% of my money! Dividends are not irrelevant.

People who are familiar with my work are aware that my preference for good dividend paying equities goes back many years. There are numerous arguments in favour of dividend investing. Some of the most frequently heard are:

- Attractive Returns: Dividend payers tend to increase in value over time.
- Less Volatility: Dividends help reduce the potential fall of a company's stock price, thereby reducing volatility.
- Increasing Yield: Companies often increase their dividends year over year.
- Favorable Tax Treatment: Canadian dividends receive more favourable tax treatment than interest income.

These are all good reasons for pursuing a dividend strategy for your investment portfolio, but as always, I like to look at the empirical evidence. So, I charted the returns from the TSX Composite stock Index (formerly the TSE 300) back 32 years and compared the overall returns including dividends, with those not including dividends. – Starting in 1982.

Chart 8.1

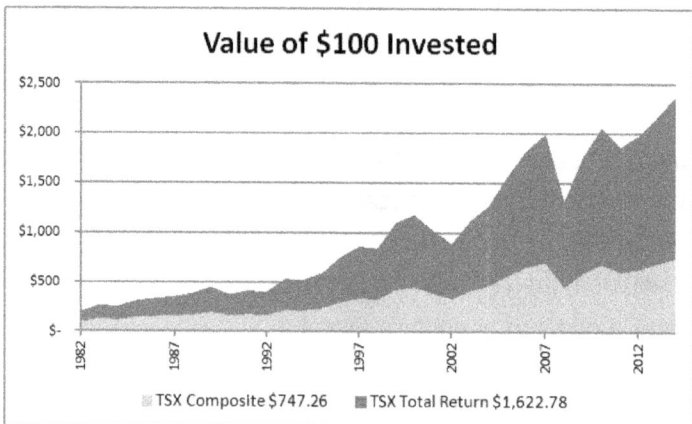

Value of $100 Invested

TSX Composite $747.26   TSX Total Return $1,622.78

By December 31, 2014, $100 invested in the stock index (not including dividends) would have turned into $747. At the same time, though, the component companies also paid out $640 in dividends, resulting in a total ending value of $1,623. In other words, dividends accounted for nearly 50% of the TSX Total Return Index over the 32-year period.

Even more remarkably, I traced the data back to 1957, when the index was devised as the TSE 300 and found that by the end of 2011, $100 invested in the TSX Composite Price Index grew to be $1,705.79 over the 55-year stretch. But add in the dividends, and your investment grows to $7,847.75. – That's 4.6 times $1,705.79! In other words, dividends accounted for 78% of the total returns generated by the TSX Total Return Index. For this illustration, however, I use the 32-year data, so that in making certain comparisons, I am able to compare apples to apples.

I have long been an advocate of investing, not just in companies that pay dividends, but particularly in companies that pay above-average dividends, and have the capacity to, and a record of increasing those dividends over time.

So, for comparative purposes, I have prepared the following charts which illustrate the dividends paid, and the total returns for three of the highest dividend paying companies of the 100 largest companies trading on the Toronto Stock Exchange back to 1982[2]. The companies are Enbridge Inc., Fortis Inc, and TD Banking group. I chose these particular companies because:

1.   They all pay above-average dividends.

2.   They all have a record of increasing those dividends.

3.   They represent three different industries.

Enbridge Inc.

Enbridge is an oil and gas pipeline company that transports crude oil and natural gas across Canada, and into the US. The company also operates a natural gas distribution company which provides distribution services in Ontario, Quebec, New Brunswick and New York State.

Chart 8.2

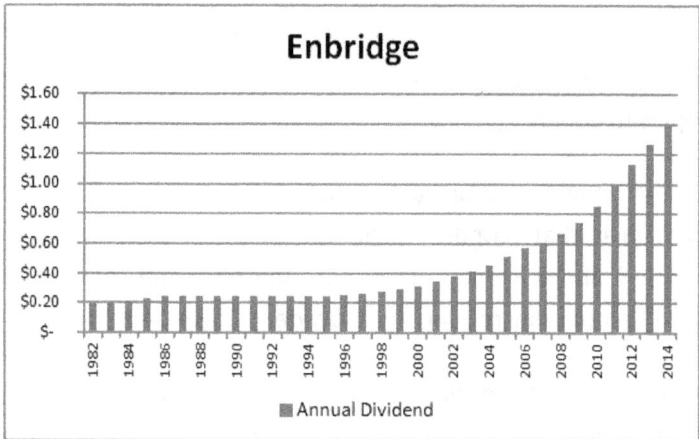

Adjusted for share splits, Enbridge paid a 20 cent dividend in 1982, and gradually increased it (more noticeably from the mid-90's on), and in 2014, the company paid a dividend of 1.40_3$.

Chart 8.3

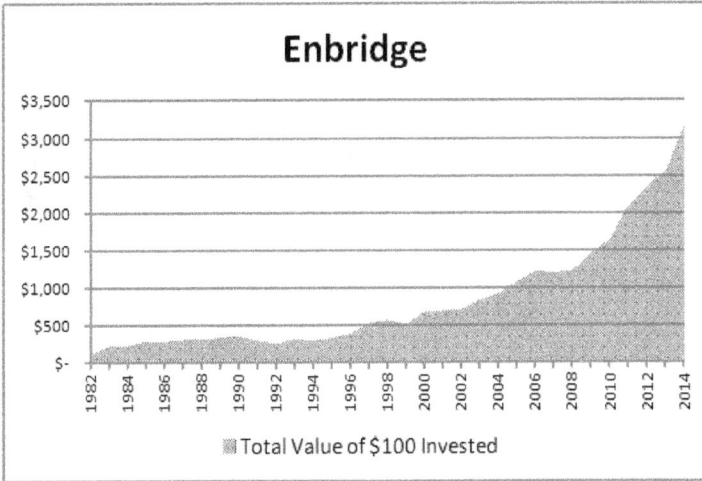

Enbridge

Total Value of $100 Invested

Enbridge stock has responded accordingly. $100 invested in Enbridge common shares in 1982 would be worth $2,515 at the end of 2014 (including dividends)[4].

Fortis Inc.

Fortis Inc. is a Canadian utility company which operates electric utilities in five Canadian provinces and two Caribbean countries and a natural gas utility in British Columbia. The company owns non-regulated generation assets, primarily hydroelectric, across Canada and in Belize and Upper New York State, as well as hotels and commercial office and retail space in Canada.

Chart 8.4

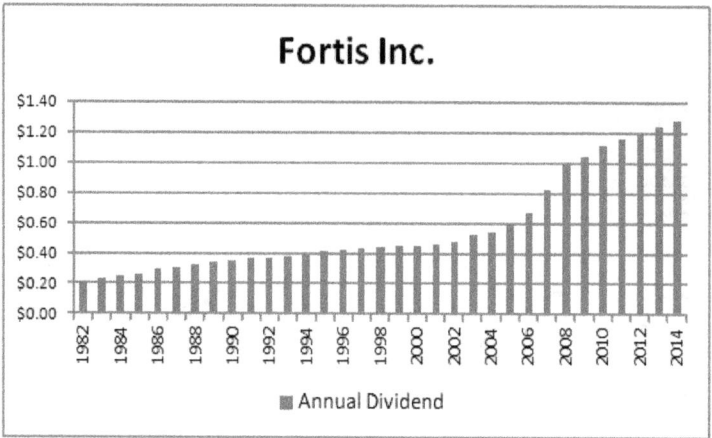

Fortis Inc.

Annual Dividend

In 1982, Fortis paid a dividend of 21 cents per share, and as the following chart illustrates, the company steadily increased that dividend, so that it now pays $1.28 in dividends5.

Chart 8.5

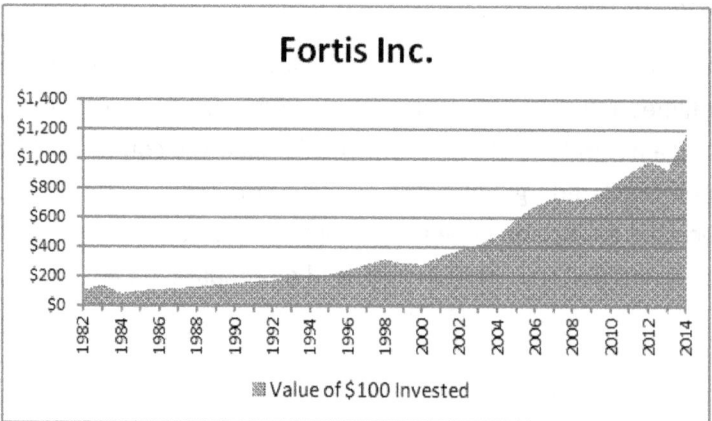

Fortis Inc.

Value of $100 Invested

The happy result of this steady progress has resulted in very respectable stock returns. $100 invested in Fortis stock in 1982 would have turned into $1,181 by the end of 2014 (including dividends)6.

These charts certainly illustrate one of the more popular characteristics of dividend stocks, which is a tendency toward less volatility than the overall market. But note also that even for a particular company, there is a tendency for the rate of overall returns to have a close correlation with the rate of dividend increases.

TD Bank Group

The Toronto-Dominion Bank Group, better known to consumers as TD Canada Trust serves approximately 20.5 million customers operating in a number of locations in financial centres worldwide. TD paid an adjusted dividend in 1982 of 16 cents per share and increased that dividend in all but four of the next 30 years. Adjusted for stock splits, the bank paid $3.68 per share in dividends in 2014; by far the most significant increase over the 30-year period, of the companies reviewed7.

Chart 8.6

TD Canada Trust

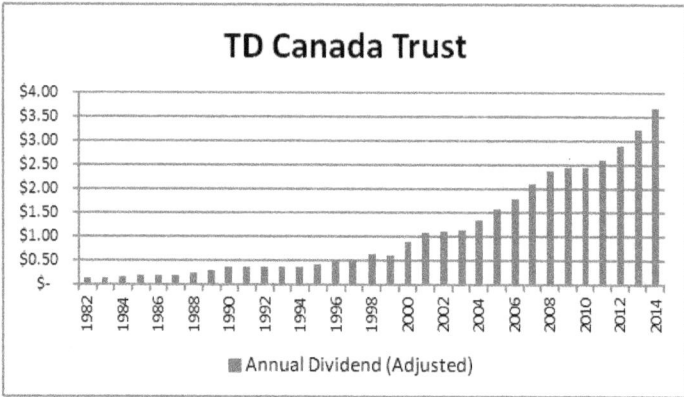

Annual Dividend (Adjusted)

As one might predict then, TD shares have provided even better returns than the former two examples. $100 invested in TD common shares in 1984 would be worth $4,180 at the end of 2014 (including dividends)[8].

Chart 8.7

TD Canada Trust

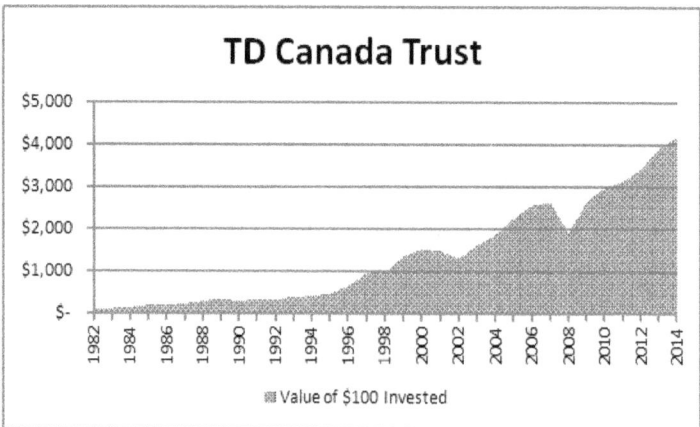

Value of $100 Invested

These are all fine examples of successful enterprises, but to make it all really meaningful, we should compare them to companies that have not fit the description of those that pay above-average dividends, and have the capacity to, and a record of increasing those dividends over time. So, I checked up on the 25 biggest publicly traded companies from back in 1982 and listed them according to their dividend yield. I chose the top 25, because Enbridge, Fortis and TD Bank are all large caps, and after all, we want to compare apples to apples.

No Dividends:

It turns out four of these large caps didn't pay any dividends at all. Of these four, none still exists in its former state. Holders of Ford Motor Company of Canada were the luckiest of the lot. Ford Canada traded at $40.25 at the end of 1982 and was bought out by the US parent company in 1995 for $185 per share. $100 in Ford Canada stock got you $459.63 in that span[9].

Chrysler Canada holders were not so lucky. Chrysler attached itself to, then was cut loose from Daimler-Benz, and went bankrupt in 2009. Your $100 went up in smoke[10].

Canada Development Corporation (CDC) traded at $6.00 in 1982. The company underwent a series of mergers and takeovers that eventually potted holders $15.28 in cash and a ¼ share of TransCanada Corporation. Net worth on December 31, 2011, was $26.86. Your $100 worth of CDC in 1982 translated to $447.67 by the end of 2011[11].

The fourth non-dividend payer in our group was *Dome Petroleum*. Dome traded at $9.00 per share in 1982, and aside from paying no dividends, the company was carrying a lot of debt. Dome was taken over as a distressed company in 1988 by Amoco Petroleum for $1.14 per share[12].

Low Dividends:

Of the three next lowest dividend payers among the largest companies in 1982, Alcan Aluminum traded at $34.50. The stock split 3 for 2 in both 1987 and 1989, resulting in shareholders having 2.25 shares for each single share they held in 1982. Alcan was taken over by Rio Tinto in 2007 for $101.00 per share, bringing in $227.25 to any-one who held one share in 1982. So a $100 investment in Alcan in 1982 brought in $658.70 plus about $40 in dividends, or $698.70 in total[13]. This is better than CDC or Dome, but still not in the same class as Fortis, Enbridge or TD Bank.

The next two in the lower dividend category are Loblaw Companies, and Simpson-Sears (now Sears Canada Ltd). – Finally, a pair of companies that are still around!

Loblaw Companies:

In 1982, Loblaws was Canada's largest grocery chain. Revenues were nearly $5.8 Billion, and the company netted over $52 million in profits. But earnings were not consistent, and the dividend yield was mediocre at best, at only 2.3%. (By comparison, Bell Canada yielded over 8%.) The stock traded at $9.62 to close out 1982, and the dividend was 22 cents.

As the chart below indicates, the dividend was reduced to conserve cash, and reduced again, and it was reflected in the stock performance. In the mid- to-late 1990's, Loblaws earnings improved, and the company began boosting its dividend which also is reflected in stock performance. In fact, virtually all of the returns from this stock over a period of 30 years occurred between 1997 and 2004; a period when the company was steadily increasing its dividend[14]. When the company stopped bumping its dividend in 2006, the stock languished until it started increasing it again in 2013.

Chart 8.8

Loblaw Companies

$1.20	
$1.00	
$0.80	
$0.60	
$0.40	
$0.20	
$-	

1982 1984 1986 1988 1990 1992 1994 1996 1998 2000 2002 2004 2006 2008 2010 2012 2014

▇ Dividends Paid

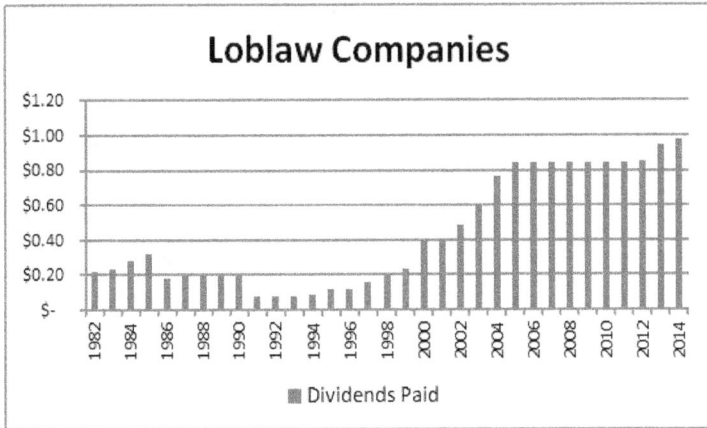

In the 32 years between 1982 and the end of 2014, Loblaws increased their dividend from 22 cents to 98 cents, but it did get cut a few times before resuming its growth. $100 invested in Loblaws shares in 1982 would be worth $1,277 (including dividends) by the end of 2014[15]. Notice the same trend as before.

Chart 8.9

Loblaw Companies

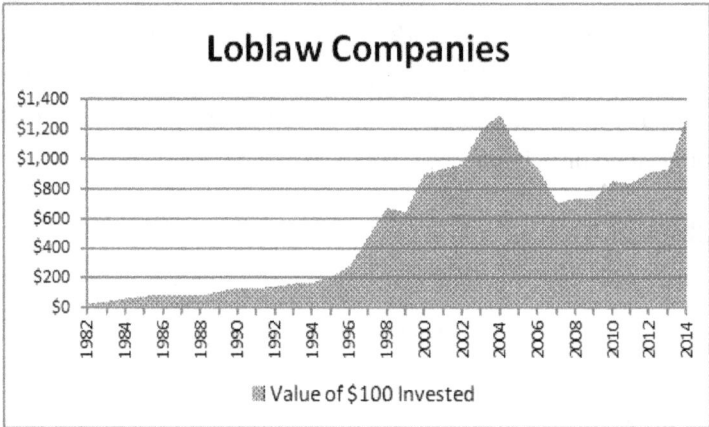

Value of $100 Invested

During periods when dividend increases have stalled, or been reduced, the stock languished. In periods when dividend growth was strong, so, too, was the overall stock return.

Simpson Sears:

Our remaining low dividend-payer of the "big 25" was Simpson Sears, which later became Sears Canada. Sears traded at $7.25 in 1982 and paid a dividend of 20 cents.

Chart 8.10

Sears Canada

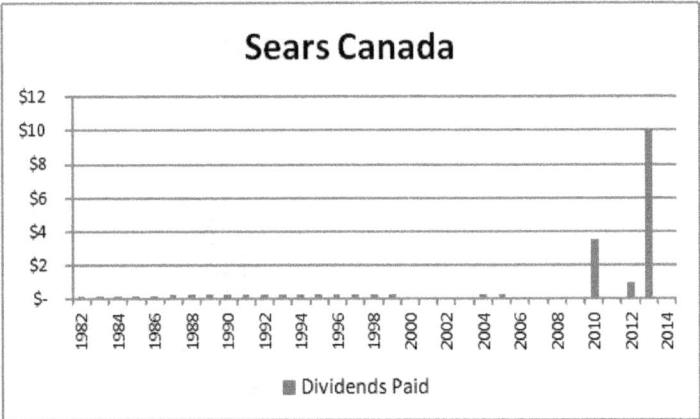

The dividend was bumped to 21 cents in 1987, then to 24 cents in 1988, where it stayed until being cut altogether in 2000. It was re-instated in 2003 for a while, then stopped again, until a special dividend was declared in 2010 of $3.50 soon after US parent Sears Holdings Corp. accumulated just over 90 per cent of the company. As well, Sears paid out $1.00 in 2012 and $10.00 per share in 2013, as the company sold off assets[16].

Chart 8.11

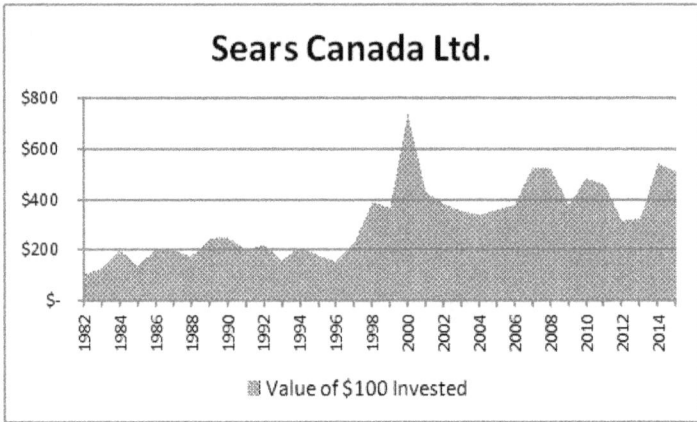

Sears Canada Ltd.

Value of $100 Invested

In all, Sears Canada has had a very mediocre dividend record, and it is reflected by a mediocre stock return. At the end of 2014, your $100 investment in Sears Canada grew to only $509.17[17].

Conclusions:

The companies reviewed in this report were not chosen at random, or because they conveniently make the "point" I am trying to convey. The higher dividend companies were chosen because they exhibit the characteristics of what I consider quality investments, as demonstrated by their high representation in the portfolios I managed. The non-dividend companies are actually the only four non-dividend payers out of the twenty-five largest publicly-traded Canadian companies at the beginning of our period of review, and the low-dividend payers were the actual lowest dividend payers from that same group.

Clearly, the high-dividend payers out-performed the low-dividend payers by a long-shot, and the non-dividend payers... well, on the whole, they were a bust.

If there was any doubt about the value of an investment strategy that is centered around investing not just in companies that pay dividends, but particularly in companies that pay above-average dividends, and have the capacity to, and a record of increasing those dividends over time; then that doubt should be completely erased by now.

But is this enough? Can we simply just load up on the highest dividend-payers and forget about it? There are a lot of dividend devotees out there who would say "Yeah, that's about it." Well, don't believe them. If it were that easy, every-one would be doing it. Just like any investment strategy, there are caveats and exceptions that can jump out and bite you in the behind.

Back in 2008, there was a certain T-V personality who seemed to jump on the dividend band-wagon, spouting the phrase: "PAAAAY DADDY!" ...with all the confidence, charisma and pomp he could muster[18]. He took a shining to a company called Dian Shipping Co.(DSX) which was listed on the New York Stock Exchange and traded at about $30 per share at the time[19]. One of my clients called to ask why he didn't hold DSX in his portfolio because the guy on T-V says they are a great company, and it pays a 10% (yes, ten percent!) dividend.

The very first thing I checked was this company's dividend coverage. The dividend coverage is the ratio by which a company's earnings exceeds its dividend. I very quickly discovered the company had been paying out more in dividends that it was earning for the past three years – and was expected to do the same again in 2008[20]. There are only a few things that can happen when a company pays out more in dividends than it is earning, and none of them are good. By the fourth quarter of 2008, DSX was forced to eliminate its dividend, and the stock eventually bottomed out at around $6.00 per share. Thank goodness I talked my client out of investing in Dian Shipping!

Remember the market collapse of late 2008 – early 2009? I found it so ironic that this same T-V guy went on and on about the dangers of owning shares in the "big six" Canadian banks. Because each of the "big six" had taken significant write-downs on their toxic mortgage securities from the US, "Canadian banks" he said, "have to cut their dividends; there is no way around it."[21]

I have to admit I found this a little incredulous. It sure looked like several journalists were doing a little sensationalizing, or at the very least, slipping into panic mode. A little research revealed the highest dividend payout ratio among the big six was the Bank of Montreal, at 74% - meaning BMO was paying out about 74% of its net earnings in dividends. Granted, the bank normally paid out around 60%, but the temporary hit to earnings caused a "blip" in the payout as a percentage. The others were all less than 60%.

At around this time, the World Economic forum reported that it considered Canada's banks the safest in the world. Canadian regulators required our banks to maintain a Tier 1 Capital Ratio (equity capital and disclosed reserves as a percentage of credit exposures) of at least 7.0% in order to protect customer deposits. As at January 31, 2009, the banks' capital ratios were as follows:

- BMO: 10.2%
- BNS: 9.5%
- CIBC: 10.1%
- Royal Bank: 10.6%
- TD: 10.1%
- National Bank: 10.0%

Clearly, balance sheets for all of the "Big Six" far exceeded federal guidelines[22]. As well, during that quarter, all six major Canadian banks exceeded analysts' earnings estimates.

I also checked the dividend history back to pre-depression days and found that with the exception of National Bank, not one major Canadian bank had cut dividends since World War Two, when the federal government requested banks cut back operations to conserve manpower for the war effort. National cut its dividend in 1981, then suspended it altogether in 1982. It was reinstated in 1983. It was cut again when the bank ran into difficulty in 1992 but has remained steady since that time[23].

My report to clients in March 2009 advised them not just to continue holding their bank shares, but to take the opportunity presented them by the depressed market by adding to their positions. By December 2014, the TSX Composite Index had doubled from those March 2009 lows. An equity investment divided equally between the six big bank shares in March 2009 was worth more than triple its original cost by the end of 2014. I'll take triple over double any time.

The most important things to take away from this chapter are:

A:) Dividends do matter. Investment returns for higher dividend paying stocks are usually significantly better than no or low dividend payers.

B:) Have a look at the company's dividend history. The stars shine much brighter for companies that have a track record of continually increasing their dividends.

C:) A high dividend alone does not necessarily make a good investment. Make sure the company has the earnings to support the dividend it is paying. If it doesn't, there is some likelihood the dividend will soon be cut.

D:) For Heaven's sake, take the babble coming out of the mouths of so-called experts on T-V with a grain of salt. They like to stir things up. Controversy sells advertising.

I'll leave you with a final consideration. While putting a strong emphasis on dividends when building your investment portfolio, it would be a mistake to just look at dividend yields in a vacuum. There are a couple of other concepts that deserve review, and have a high correlation with superior investment returns. These are the Price/Earnings Ratio and its alter-ego the Earnings/Price Ratio (Earnings Yield) as well as the Price/Book Value. Let's have a look at these concepts in the following chapters.

Chapter 9

The P/E Effect and Earnings Yield

Of all the measures and ratios used to assess the value of a common stock or even the overall market, the P/E Ratio is easily the most recognized. The Price/Earnings (P/E) ratio is simply the market price of a company divided by the company's earnings per share. If a company's shares are trading at $30.00 and it earned $2.50 per outstanding share over the last 12 months, it has a P/E ratio of $30 divided by $2.50 or 12 times earnings.

The P/E Effect

As early as 1934, Ben Graham and David Dodd recognized that companies with low P/E ratios would be likely to provide better returns than higher P/E comparables in their epic book "*Security Analysis*"[1]. In 1960, S.F.Nicholson conducted a study that found that low P/E companies not only outperform high P/E companies during a long studied period but low P/E companies also beat the market at general[2]. Subsequent studies by McWilliam (1966)[3], Miller & Widmann (1966)[4], Breen (1968)[5], and Breen & Savage (1968)[6] also found somewhat same evidence as Nicholson and supported what has become known as the P/E Effect.

Those who claim the market is so efficient in pricing securities correctly that it is impossible to take advantage of "market anomalies" such as the P/E Effect, for years, refuted its very existence. In 1992, Eugene Famma and Kenneth French, pioneers of Efficient Market Theory acknowledged the P/E

Effect, but claimed its benefits are completely offset by risk factors."[7] Astonishingly their proof was that according to EMT, all excess returns to the market must be offset by risk factors. Well, in my books a stock that is trading at 12 times its annual earnings is safer than one trading at 120 times almost every time.

Graham produced a study in 1973 that compared the returns of the 10 highest P/E stocks of the 30 stock Dow Jones Industrial Index to the lowest 10 P/E stocks[8]. The study was broken down into six - 5 year periods, ending in 1969. The lower P/E stocks outperformed the Higher P/E comparables in every period; by an average of 9.2%.

Graham also calculated the results of investing $ 10,000 in either the high- or low-multiple groups in the Dow Jones Industrial Average in 1937 and switching every five years into the highest P/ Es (in the first case) and the lowest P/ Es (in the latter). Ten thousand dollars invested in the lowest P/ Es this way in 1937 would have increased to $ 66,866 by the end of 1962. Invested in the highest P/ Es, the $ 10,000 would have appreciated to only $25,437.

In his excellent book, "_Contrarian Investment Strategies_", David Dreman outlined several studies he had conducted throughout the 1980's and 1990's; each of them concluding that low P/E stocks outperform high P/E stocks by a large margin[9]. In one study, he broke down the largest 1800 stocks in the Compustat database into five quintiles, according to their P/E level for the period between 1963 and 1985. The group with the lowest P/E's outperformed the highest P/E group by over 10% on an annual basis. In another study, Dreman performed similar tests on 5 groups of Compustat stocks; grouped according to market cap for the twenty-one years ending 1989. He found that the P/E effect held up regardless of the size of the company.

In his classic "_Stocks for the Long Run_", Jeremy Siegel broke the S&P 500 down into quintiles according to P/E ratios, and demonstrated that $1.00 invested in the highest P/E group in 1957 grew to $64 by the end of 2012, while $1.00 invested in the lowest P/E group grew to $800 in the same period[10].

Evidence supporting the P/E effect over the long term is so pervasive, it seems many investors have come to depend on P/E as the only measure they use when assessing the suitability of a stock purchase. This is especially true of analysts and so-called experts who should really know better, but often get caught up in the excitement of an over-reaching stock market. All too many times I have heard a high stock valuation justified because: "When you compare ABC stock, at 21 times earnings to the market at 24 times, it looks pretty attractive." But comparing a P/E only to the overall market instead of the company's own history and track record is a misuse of the P/E effect concept. And it is a misuse that can get you into serious trouble.

Even comparing a company's P/E to its own track record is not infallible. Can you just buy the lowest P/E stocks, and hold onto them forever – guaranteeing you superior returns? The answer is no. Not now. Not ever. The P/E Effect appears to prevail the vast majority of the time, but, as with any other predictive tool, there will be times when it may not work – when things are "different". The period from 2005 to 2009 was a perfect example of one of those times.

Remembering that several massive household-name companies (financial and otherwise) fell into the abyss during the 2008-2009 global financial crisis, I reviewed the stocks that make up the Dow Jones Industrial Average (DJIA) in a similar manner as Ben Graham has many years before for the years 2004-2009, and 2010-2014[11].

And, sure enough, the 2004-2009 period showed a break in the pattern. The 10 stocks with the lowest P/E's at the beginning of the period lost a total of 8.4% after dividends during the period while the 10 stocks with the highest P/E's returned a total of 127.6%. To be sure, most of the low P/E stocks did better, but of the top ten, three companies had disastrous results. In 2009, General Motors went bankrupt resulting in 84% loss after dividends. And financial stalwarts AIG, and Citigroup lost 94% and 79% of their values respectively. Returns like this can really skew overall results.

Fortunately, for the 2010-2014 period things normalized significantly. The best of the low P/E stocks, Kraft Foods, beat the best of the high P/E stocks by 140%. Over the 5 year stretch, the 10 low P/E stocks returned 991% collectively, compared to 714% for the high P/E stocks.

Does the 2004-2009 break from the norm invalidate the P/E Effect? Absolutely not! What it does, however, is emphasize that you can never put your portfolio on "auto-pilot". A low price to earnings ratio is often an indicator of a staid, reliable company that has a long history of slow, steady earnings growth. But it might mean something else. It could mean that investors are wary of a company's ability to maintain current earnings because of company-specific issues or fundamental cyclicality.

General Motors had the lowest P/E ratio of all Dow 30 stocks in 2004, having earned $4.95 per $40.00 share (after earning $7.14/sh in 2003). Five years later it was bankrupt. Before it came to a head in 2009, GM lost $5.67/share in 2005, $3.50 in 2006, $0.04 in 2007 and a whopping $29.00 per share in 2008. Clearly there were signs of trouble ahead, and many investors avoided the stock, resulting in the low P/E. Even for those who missed the early signs, and bought or kept the stock in 2004, there was plenty of time to sell before disaster struck in 2009[12].

Citigroup was the next lowest P/E stock among the 2004 group, with AIG Financial not far behind it. Financial stocks were decimated during the global 2008-2009 financial crisis, which began with the US housing bubble, and the implosion of the (toxic) mortgage-backed Collateral-Debt Obligation (CDO) market[13]. This is the same financial crisis that took most of Wall Street by surprise. Yet, there were signs.

In 2006, AIG stopped selling credit protection on CDO's[14] (AIG survived the crisis.), but Merrill Lynch fired a group of analysts for making a presentation warning about the dangers of the CDO market. (Merrill Lynch did not survive.) In 2007 Century Financial went bankrupt, Bear Stearns had to halt redemptions on some of their CDO backed hedge funds, Country Wide Financial went bankrupt, and the US government had to prop up Federal Home Loan Mortgage Corporation (Freddy Mac) and Federal National Mortgage Association (Fanny Mae)[15].

It all finally sank in late 2008, when the Feds had to take over Freddy Mac and Fanny Mae, Lehman Brothers, and when

Wachovia Bank and Washington Mutual (among others) went bankrupt. Merrill Lynch had to be taken over by Bank of America, and Citigroup barely escaped failure with the help of government aid.[16] That's when the proverbial dung hit the fan.

But the signs were there. And most people - whether it be dealers too busy making scads of money in the short term (see Merrill Lynch, above) or regular investors, emotionally attached and afraid of missing out – just could not see those signs – or could not connect the dots.

The thing is, you don't have to have advanced degrees in finance or economics to recognize when you should be selling your position in a stock. All you really have to do is set your parameters before you purchase, and stick to your plan. The emphasis is on sticking to your plan.

In 2005, GM lost $5.67/share, and the stock no longer qualified as a low P/E stock. That's when the shares should have been sold. In 2007, Citicorp earnings fell to $7.20/share and the P/E rose to 41 times earnings. In the same year, AIG earnings fell 40%, to $71.60/share, and the P/E climbed over 16 times earnings. These stocks no longer qualified as low P/E stocks either, and should have been sold in 2007[17].

"It's General Motors," you tell yourself. "Surely I can cut it a little slack!" "Wachovia Bank? A solid blue-chipper... Merryl Lynch – been around for a hundred years.... Surely they deserve some leeway... they will turn it around" These thoughts are fueled by emotion; and when it comes to managing your investments, emotion is your worst enemy. You can never just buy, and hold forever, without establishing some kind of "checks and balances" if you expect to stay ahead of the market.

These checks and balances begin with a review of past earnings. The automotive industry is notoriously cyclical. An auto manufacturer may report modest earnings or even a loss at the early stages of a business cycle, but as the economy expands, earnings gradually increase, peaking just as the economy does. Then, being a big-ticket item, sales fall dramatically, followed by earnings, which may again, fall into negative territory. Investors expect this, and know that the longer the economic cycle has gone on, the nearer it is to its end, and the nearer the auto manufacturer is to its inevitable earnings decline.

As a result, investors are less willing to pay a premium multiple for automotive earnings at the peak of a business cycle. The same could be said of oil companies and mining shares. In fact, mining companies' earnings can be so volatile that they may trade at extremely low P/E's at the peak of the cycle, and (assuming they still report positive earnings) at triple digit P/E's when the market is at its lowest.

The bottom line is, if a company does not exhibit steady, regular earnings, it is not likely a good candidate for a P/E Effect strategy. Otherwise, stocks tend to revert to their mean P/E.

Since 1936, the S&P 500 Index has traded at an average price/earnings multiple of a little over 16 times earnings. As the economy goes through a typical business cycle, recession gives way to recovery, which in turn becomes expansion, until eventually contraction and recession take over, and we start all over again. As the recovery and expansion phases go on, earnings tend to grow, and the market with them.

Chart 9.1

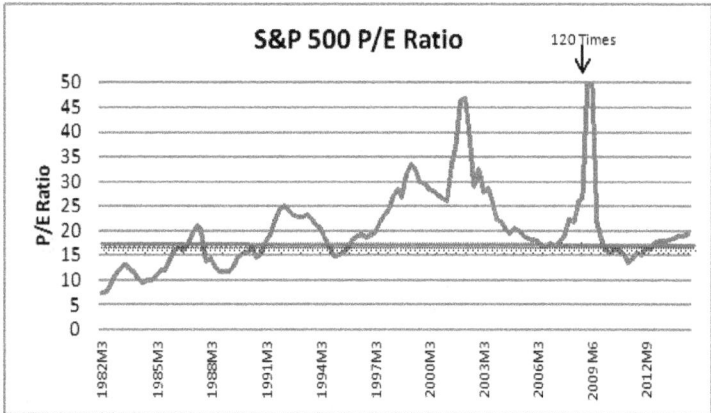

Chart 9.1 shows the annual P/E ratio for the S&P 500 since 1936, with the red line depicting the mean value of about 16.5 times earnings[18].

Collective per-share earnings have gradually increased since 1936 from under $20 to over $100, according to data provided by Robert Schiller. As the rate of growth increased in the 1980's and 1990's, P/E multiples increased as well; no doubt, in contemplation of higher future earnings.

Over the last 25 years, we can see that P/E levels have twice become stratospheric. Earnings expectations leading up to the market meltdown in 2000 became unrealistic as part of the "tech bubble". Business, however, has a knack for dashing those hopes from time to time, and as earnings took a hit, P/E levels returned to more "normal" values.

In 2008, the spike was not related so much to over-zealous stock purchasers, but rather to the bursting of a real estate bubble in the US, and the price implosion for mortgage and other financial instruments. Even non-financial companies lost confidence, causing corporate earnings to evaporate. It took a 54% decline to bring prices back in line before earnings began their gradual recovery.

There are two messages here; the first is that stock prices get out of whack for different reasons. Remember, the P/E ratio has two components. The price component may become inflated as a result of unrealistic expectations, or as Alan Greenspan would say, "irrational exuberance" while the earnings component may become temporarily depressed as a result of cyclical or other factors. The second message is that no matter how out of whack they may get, given time, stock P/E ratios tend to revert to the mean.

Now, this is where I endeavor to turn the P/E Ratio around – quite literally. At the start of this chapter, I said that of all the measures and ratios used to assess the value of a common stock, the P/E Ratio is easily the most recognized. And that's understandable; it's easy to calculate; it makes it easy to compare a company's valuation to the overall market, to other stocks, and to its own historical valuation.

But the concept of price – earnings multiple also has some flaws. For example, what happens when a company reports a loss on its income statement? Can a stock have a negative P/E?

What if ABC Corp. reported a loss of 25¢ per share after taking a loss on a bad investment. Now it is generally expected the company will recover from its losses, and the stock is trading at $15 per share. However, take a $15 stock, and divide it by -0.25 and you come up with -60….. (minus sixty) times earnings. It kind of implies some-one might demand $60 just to take your ABC stock off your hands!

Clearly, that is a deal you are not likely to make.

If that dilemma wasn't enough to turn you off using P/E as your point of reference, consider that the magnitude of a company's loss per share will have a reverse effect than the magnitude of positive earnings. Let's say the losses at ABC Corp. deepened, and a 25¢ loss became a $1.50 loss. Now the stock is trading at minus 10 times earnings. It doesn't sound as bad, does it? Yet losses have multiplied by six. And should you want to average the company's P/E Ratio over time, this negative P/E effect can skew the average beyond reality, and render the calculation useless.

So, when analysts come across a negative earnings situation, they simply put "N/A" where the otherwise negative P/E would be. The problem with that is it makes it very difficult for those same analysts to draw up a proper graph or chart (something they love to do!) with a bunch of "N/A"s all over it.

Another issue with using the P/E multiple as your principal valuation tool is that it doesn't directly comment on your likely return. 30 times earnings seems quite expensive when compared to the overall market at 20 times. Likewise, 15 times looks pretty cheap for a stock that usually trades at 18 times, and is particularly cheap compared to stocks of similar companies trading at 21 times earnings. But what kind of return is does it imply for you?

Earnings Yield:

The answer is much simpler than you might think. Just turn the formula around – and it solves both problems. Instead of looking at the P/E ratio, look at the E/P ratio. The E/P Ratio is also known as the earnings yield. If a stock trades at $50/share, and the company produces $2.50 per share in earnings, the P/E multiple is 50/2.50 or 20 times earnings. Instead of working out the P/E, we want to determine the Earnings Yield, so instead, we divide $2.50 by $50 and come up with .05 (or 5.0%).

Here is why knowing the Earnings Yield is so important: If I buy XYZ Corp. for $100 per share, and the stock pays a $3.00 dividend, clearly my dividend yield is 3.0%. Assuming XYZ has earnings per share (EPS) of $6.00 per share, I also know my Earnings Yield is 6.0%. That is the total of what the company paid out to me in dividends and the amount it re-invested on my behalf. That's information I want to know – and information the P/E on its own doesn't tell me directly.

Now I can compare my earnings yield to other stocks, to the overall market, as well as to other potential investments. The following chart compares the S&P 500 Earnings Yield to 10 Year US Government bonds from 1961 to 2014[19]. The average bond yield for that period was 6.4% while the average SP500 Earnings Yield was 6.6%.

Chart 9.2

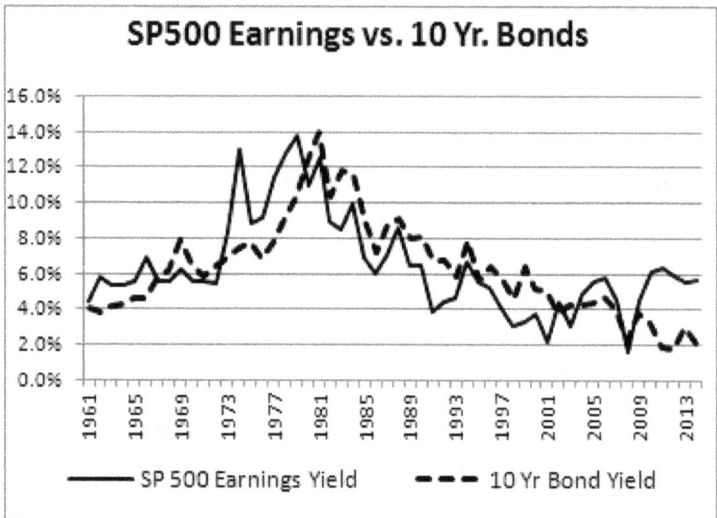

Note how closely these two yields have tracked each other for more than 50 years. There was a period in the mid-1970's when the earnings yield moved up significantly higher than the bond yield, but that corrected itself not so much with the short-lived stock rally in 1977, but rather with the longer-lasting increase in bond yields that followed. The two had since not digressed to that extent until recently, and I (as do many) expect this divergence will also be corrected by increasing bond yields eventually.

As discussed in the chapter on choosing your asset mix, as interest rates increase, bond prices decline. This leads me to the conclusion that at a time when stock earnings yields exceed bond yields by nearly 3.5%, equities make a pretty good investment.

The final advantage of using Earnings Yield as a measure over P/E is that should a company fall into a loss position on its income statement, it is indeed possible to show a negative earnings yield. A $50 stock that has lost $1.00/share, for example, has a -2% earnings yield. No need to use "N/A" in your analysis.

Recall that our definition of a market is a compilation of all the different securities that are traded as a part of that market. Each of these securities should be valued (mostly) on its own individual merits and it is the individual securities that go into your portfolio we are interested in putting a value on. So, let's turn our focus away from the overall market, and towards some individual securities.

Enbridge is one of the companies we favored in our discussion on dividends.

Chart 9.3

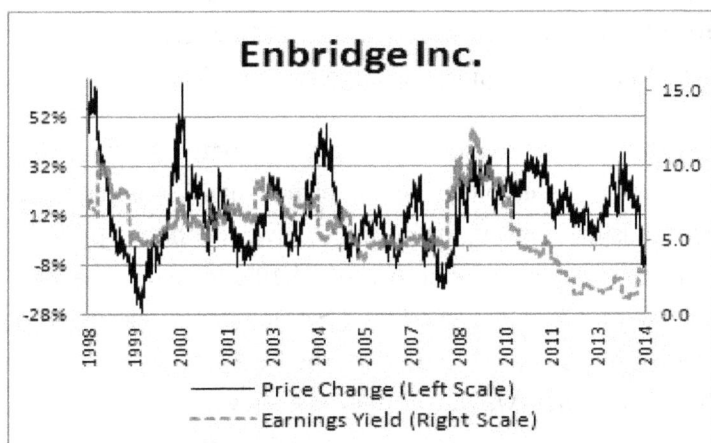

At the onset of my dividend review, Enbridge was:

- among the 25 largest public companies in Canada,
- among the top dividend payers on the TSE 300,
- had a track record of increasing its dividend regularly and
- had sufficient earnings to afford the dividends it was paying.

Enbridge proved to be one of the best performing stocks in our review, so It seems fitting to compare year-over-year stock performance to its Earnings Yield as well.

It turns out between 1996 and 2014 Enbridge provided an average earnings yield of 6.28% (a P/E multiple of about 16 times). The average stock price gain during this period was 17.8%, or about 2.85 times the earnings yield. Chart 9.3[20] illustrates this relationship. Notice how the price performance rarely deviates too far from the 2.85 relationship; and then only for short bursts. That is, until about mid-2011, when a robust stock price and a squeeze on earnings created a wider spread than usual. Note also that in 2014 improved earnings, and a sluggish stock price has restored the balance.

This chart clearly demonstrates that it is better to invest in a stock when it's earnings yield is higher than its average than when it is low. During the period reviewed, Enbridge provided an average annual capital gain of 24.10% following the 2427 observations that the earnings yield equaled or exceeded its average of 6.22% and 11.90% for the 2526 observations when the earnings yield was lower than its average.

In fact, when we break the earnings yield down into quartiles between the highest and lowest observations for earnings yield during this period, the highest quartile resulted in an average stock gain of 42.44%, and while the chart also indicates there may be merit in selling the stock when the yield is at extreme lows, even investors buying in the bottom quartile saw capital appreciation of 8.05% on average.

As always, I also like to review comparables in order to provide contrast, and in my dividend analysis, I also reviewed the track record for Loblaw Companies.

Loblaws does indeed provide a contrast from Enbridge shares. At the onset of my review, Loblaw was:

- among the 25 largest public companies in Canada, but was:
- one of the lower dividend payers on the TSE 300,
- had a spotty track record with regard to increasing its dividend and
- had an inconsistent earnings record.

Chart 9.4

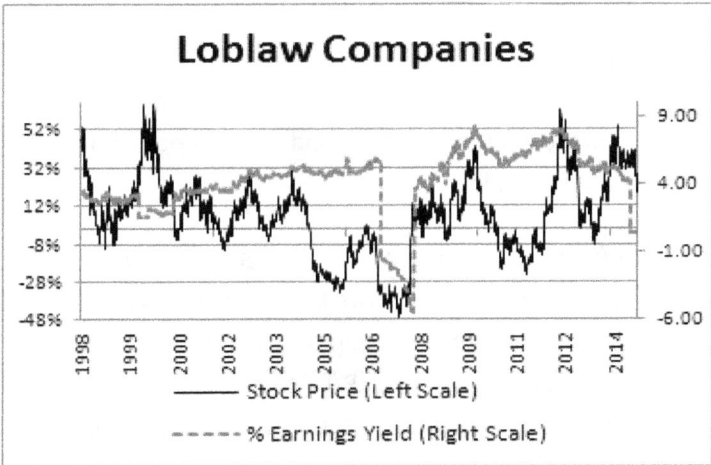

Loblaw Companies

Stock Price (Left Scale)

— — — % Earnings Yield (Right Scale)

Chart 9.4[21] shows that stock performance and earnings yield don't have quite the same relationship as for Enbridge, either.

Between 1998 and 2014 Loblaws provided an average earnings yield of 4.2%. The average stock price gain during this period was 6.6% or about 1.57 times the earnings yield. This is quite a bit lower than the Enbridge results and appear to be the price of inconsistency. In keeping with the "contrast" theme, Loblaws actually produces an average capital return of just 5.49% for the 2530 observations when the earnings yield was equal to or higher than its average of 4.22%, less than the 8.20% provided for the 1676 observations when the earnings yield was less than the average.

Rejecting the idea that Loblaw investors prefer lower profits, we can only conclude that this paradox is a direct result of unpredictability. When broken down into quartiles, the top quartile provided 6.82% capital growth while the lowest quartile resulted in an average loss of 30.2%.

There are several lessons we can learn from this data.

- Firstly, even though the price/earnings relationship in most commonly viewed as a P/E multiple, it is often more useful to flip it around to E/P and see it as the Earnings Yield.

- Second, low P/E - high earnings yield stocks usually provide superior returns than high P/E, low earnings yield stocks, but it is important to look a little below the surface. A low P/E could be the result of inconsistent, unpredictable or declining earnings.

- It is better to compare P/E levels to past results from the same company rather than to the overall market. A high P/E-low earnings yield is not a good investment just because the market may be over-priced.

- It can be worthwhile to sell a stock when the earnings yield is low and buy it back when the earnings yield has declined. This will depend on the reason for the change. If the stock price has just risen in the overall excitement of a bull market, you should consider selling. But if the earnings yield is low (P/E is high) because earnings have fallen off, you may need to determine why earnings are down, and satisfy yourself that it is only temporary before you buy it back.

- It is much easier to pursue the above strategy for companies that usually exhibit steady, predictable earnings growth.

Chapter 10

Price to Book Value

Another popular measure for many fundamental analysts is a stock's price to book value (P/BV). Most companies include the book value per share in their financial statements, and if they don't it is not a difficult ratio to calculate.

A balance sheet starts out by listing all assets, then subtracts liabilities – as well as the value of preferred shares, and comes up with a value of equity "attributable to common shares". Let's say that value is $100 million. If the company has 10 million shares outstanding, its book value per share is $10.00. And if the stock is trading at $20.00 per share, it is trading at two times book value.

There are several advantages of using price to book value to gauge a stock's relative value compared to other measures. For example, it is much more stable than using price/earnings or price/cash flow because it essentially represents the cumulative results of the company's operations. Current earnings and cash flow results can be much more volatile as the economy goes through a business cycle.

2008 started off with oil priced at about $90 per barrel, and prices were on the rise. It peaked in July 2008 at just over $140 and fell to barely $40 by early 2009. This kind of volatility can play havoc with even the biggest of oil companies, and the year 2009 saw Exxon's earnings per share fall 54%, to $3.98 from $8.69 in 2008[1].

The Exxon share price closed out 2008 at $79.83, or 9.2 times earnings. By the end of 2009, the share price was 15% lower, at $68.19, so it now traded at 17.1 times earnings. In spite of the dramatic fall in earnings, the stock price held up fairly well. Since earnings were still positive, Exxon's book value per share (BVPS) actually increased during 2009, from $22.70 to $23.39. So, Price to Book declined just 20% from 3.5 times to 2.8 times; which seems pretty reasonable, compared to 4.3 times for the Dow 30 (DJIA) overall[2].

Should the Exxon share price fall because of a temporary decline in earnings? Certainly. But it should in part, reflect the value of the company's assets. And that is what we have seen in this instance.

Another advantage of using Price to Book Value is the result of the same mathematical anomaly we discussed in the chapter on Earnings Yield and the P/E Ratio. For the 10 years prior to 2012, Hewlett-Packard (HWP) traded at an average of 15.2 times earnings per share. But 2012 proved to be a tough year, and HP did some restructuring, resulting in a $6.41/share loss[3].

The HWP stock price fell from $25.76 at the start of 2012 to $13.68. Considering such a dramatic income loss, perhaps this is fitting. But from the perspective of price to earnings, the ratio is really incalculable. Should HWP trade at 15.2 times its actual 2012 earnings of -$6.41? If so, that means a shareholder would have to give me $97.43 for every share of HP I take off his hands. I'll take as much of that as I can get!

HWP's 2012 earnings loss also reduced BVPS from $19.59 to $11.63 or about 40%; almost as much as the 47% decline in the stock price. The end result was that HWP's Price/Book was reduced from 1.3 times BVPS to 1.1 times; a reflection of the investor uncertainty over the income loss, and clearly illustrating the superiority of the Price/BV formula over P/E in an income loss situation.

Analysts would also point out that if a company is expected to, or in the process of being "wound down" Price/BV is a more appropriate measure than P/E since future earnings are expected to be zero. However, since the typical investor is more interested in companies that are expected to provide earnings, growth and dividends, and not those who are folding up their tents, I will not make further comment.

Even though it's been a favored tool for investment icons like Benjamin Graham and Warren Buffet, price to book value has its detractors. There are a number of disadvantages to using Price/BV as a measure.

For instance, opponents point out that book value can be affected by a company's choice of accounting standards. How a company accounts for inventory depletion or recognized the value of intangible assets such as goodwill can have a significant impact on its book value. (Of course, it would be folly to assume reported earnings cannot be affected by the same choices.)

Book values can be skewed by the industry within which a company operates. An oil producer or steel manufacturer requires much more equipment and heavy assets than say........ a retailer, even though both may be high-quality companies and solid income producers. Thus, it would not be unusual to see a retailer trade at a much higher Price/BV than a manufacturing company.

Most resistance to using Price/BV as a measure of investment value tends to arise from two circumstances. One is related to inflation and the other to intangible assets.

Even in these days of relatively benign inflation, the overall increase in the price of goods can cause a company's book value to diverge from the actual market value of its assets. Consider Company "A", which bought a parcel of land twenty years ago for $10 million. The land is now worth $100 million, and last year, the company used $20 million from excess earnings to put up a new building on it. The book value of this land plus building is now $30 million. ($10 million the company paid for the land and $20 million it spent on the building.)

Company "B" raised $120 million last year through a stock offering and purchased a property similar to Company A's land for $100 million. Company "B" then put up a building identical to the Company "A" building, also at a cost of $20 million. The book value of Company B's property is now $120 million. ($100 million it paid for the land plus $20 million to put up the building.)

Which is the better investment? An investor taking a cursory glance at both balance sheets may be tempted to say Company "B" because it has a book value of $120 million compared to the book value of just $30 million for Company "A". But the truth is they are identical. In fact, I may be inclined to give the edge to Company "A" because they had the ability and wherewithal to fund its project with excess earnings rather than issuing new shares.

Intangible assets come in the form of goodwill, patents, trademarks, copyrights and other things that while important to the company, have no physical substance. The biggest problem this type of asset presents is determining what they are really worth. If a company's Research and Development department spends $10 million developing a patentable process, is it worth $10 million? What if some-one else develops a similar, exchangeable process tomorrow? Should the $10 million be written off? More importantly, will it be written off?

Goodwill arises when a company pays beyond the market value of assets to purchase another company. In 2005, Proctor and Gamble paid $57 billion to acquire Gillette. Prior to the merger, goodwill accounted for a significant portion of both P&G's balance sheet as well as that of Gillette. P&G was allowed to write up the value of Gillette's assets, helping to increase BVPS from $6.47 in 2005 to $19.33 in 2006₄.

But the bottom line was that P&G's goodwill and other intangible assets totalled $87.3 Billion. That is $68.6 <u>Billion</u>, or 268% more than its Property, Plant and Equipment. On the whole, <u>P&G's intangible assets accounted for more than 64% of its entire balance sheet</u>. P&G stock traded in the $60 range at the time of the merger, and it remained there until mid-2012 – 6 years later.

In fairness, P&G is an excellent company, and its brands are sold worldwide. From mid-2012 to the end of 2014 the share price has improved considerably, and the stock was up 65% by the end of 2014, compared to 70% for the S&P 500. Most investors, however, won't wait seven or eight years for their investments to start showing a profit.

Because of these problems, many analysts these days only consider tangible assets; leaving goodwill right out of their BVPS calculation. I think that may be a little extreme, but I always take intangibles into account and view them with a jaundiced eye. How have low P/BV performed?

Roger Ibbotson, Professor of Finance at Yale School of Management produced a study in 1986 illustrating the relationship between Price/Book Value for all stocks trading on the New York Stock Exchange between 1967 and 1984₅. The compound average annual returns were measured for each decile for the 18-year period, December 31, 1966, through December 31, 1984.

For the period, December 31, 1966, through December 31, 1984, the compound annual return for the NYSE Index as a whole was 8.6%. Table 10-a (on the following page) illustrates the results:

Table 10-a:

Decile Rank According to P/BV:

Compound Annual Return

Decile Rank According to P/BV	Compound Annual Return	Value of $1 invested 12/31/66 – 12/31/84
#1 (Lowest P/BV)	14.36%	$12.80
#2	14.4%	$12.88
#3	14.39%	$12.87
#4	12.43%	$9.26
#5	8.82%	$4.98
#6	8.36%	$4.60
#7	7.69%	$4.09
#8	5.63%	$2.83
#9	5.26%	$2.65
#10 (Highest P/BV)	6.06%	$3.06

As well, in 2011, David Dreman published a study in which he reviewed the performance of the largest 1500 stocks in the Compustat database from January 1970 to December 2010[6]. Rather than breaking his data into deciles, or ranges of 10%, Deman broke it down into quintiles or 5 groups of 20%. His findings for that period were almost identical to Ibbotson's.

Table 10-b

Quintile Rank According to P/BV	Compound Annual Return
#1 (Lowest P/BV)	14.3%
#2	12.4%
#3	11.1%
#4	9.6%
#5 (Highest P/BV)	8.1%

The overall market returned 11.6% annually during this period.

This is pretty compelling evidence, favouring low Price/Book Value stocks over the longer term. A $1,000 investment made on Jan 1, 1970, that returns 8.1% annually would have been worth $10,346 by December 31, 2010. That's a nice return. But at 14.3% annually, that $1,000 becomes $55,130! That is the difference between the lowest P/BV quintile and the highest.

I only have one issue with these studies but it is a biggie. I have yet to meet any-one who has an investment time horizon of 30 years - the duration of the Dreman study. Even the 18 years of the Ibbotson study seems like a bit of a stretch. The fact is, most people are looking for tangible returns on their investments within a 5-year period. So, I did a review of the Dow Jones Industrial Index (DJIA) for 3 consecutive 5 year periods, ending December 31, 2014[7]. Since the Dow is only 30 stocks, I divided the index into three sections; 10 low P/BV stocks, 10 mid P/BV stocks and 10 high P/BV stocks. Here are my results:

2000-2004:

For the first 5-year period, the low P/BV stocks outperformed both the mid and high P/BV groups spectacularly, due primarily to the remarkable recovery of Philip Morris as the company re-organized, and diversified its business, and as it became clearer that the company would survive the many class action lawsuits it faced.

On the strength of this, the low P/BV group achieved an average total growth of 99.5% per stock. The middle group gained 10.3% for each stock. Meanwhile, the high P/BV group lost an average 14.5% during the period. For the 5 year period, the DJIA lost 714 points or 6.2% overall. That's a decided advantage for the low P/BV stocks.

2005-2009:

In the period from Jan 1, 2005 – Dec. 31, 2009, the low P/BV group came out on top again, but not by much. This was the period that saw the bankruptcy of the big-3 automakers, and General Motors was among the low P/BV group (losing 100%). As well, aluminum manufacturer Alcoa fell on hard times, losing 58% of its value. In spite of this, the low P/BV group gained 7.3% on average during this tumultuous period.

The middle group did not fare so well. Philip Morris (renamed Altria) gave back 68% of its value and General Electric fell 58% while the group lost 13.7% on average. On the strength of IBM and Coca-Cola, the high P/BV group gained an average of 5.7%. For the period, the DJIA lost 955 points or 8.8%.

2010-2014:

During this period, the low P/BV group was led by Kraft Foods (now Mondelez), Travellers Insurance, Pfizer and a rejuvenated General Electric. Unfortunately, Bank of America and Alcoa remained in the mix, and their anaemic performance proved an anchor to overall returns. The top 10 returned an average of 53.8% for the 5-year period.

The middle P/BV group was buoyed by stellar rebounds for Disney, Home Depot, DuPont and American Express. This group provided an average return of 96.9% over the term. Even the high P/BV group fared well, returning 60.9% on average. For the 5 year period, the DJIA gained 7395 points or 71%.

What we can glean from all this data is that low P/BV stocks certainly outperform higher P/BV issues in the long-term, and tend to outperform them in the shorter to mid-term. But it is not always the case. Some stocks change from low to mid P/BV and even to high P/BV stocks. This does not indicate instability, only that the market price has risen (likely due to higher earnings).

GE, for example, was in the High P/BV group (at 11.9 times BV) in the 1999-2004 period and the stock lost 29% of its value. The price drop moved GE into the middle P/BV group (at 3.49 times BV) for the 2005-2009 period. The company struggled from an earnings perspective, and again, the stock fell; this time by 58%. This helped reduce the Price to just 1.5 times BV by the start of 2010, and the stock gained 67% in the following period.

Many of the Dow constituents have experienced similar accounts. McDonalds and Hewlett-Packard have found themselves in all three groups in the duration of the study. Both saved their best performance for the period they were in the low P/BV group. Companies like Dupont, Caterpillar American Express and Boeing fell into two of the groups at differing time periods; all performing better when the P/BV was lower.

But there were some that defied the norm. 3M, Coca-Cola, IBM and Johnson & Johnson all remained in the high P/BV group throughout, yet their stocks performed well. It is noteworthy, however that relative to its own P/BV range, each did better at lower P/BV values. And some companies with low prices relative to BV did very, very poorly. General Motors had a low P/BV before it went bankrupt. Alcoa maintained a low P/BV throughout and after the first period the stock languished.

In my own review, I tracked the Price/Book Value for several of the Canadian stocks we have talked about so far to see if there was a correlation between low P/BV and stock returns for Canadian stocks. Sure enough, there was. On average, TD Bank traded at about 2.02 times book value between 1998 and 2014. For the 2394 observations that P/BV was equal to or lower than 2.02 times, TD stock gained 28.7% in price over the ensuing year. For the 2301 observations that P/BV was higher than 2.02 times, the average price gain was 5.10%.

Chart 10.1

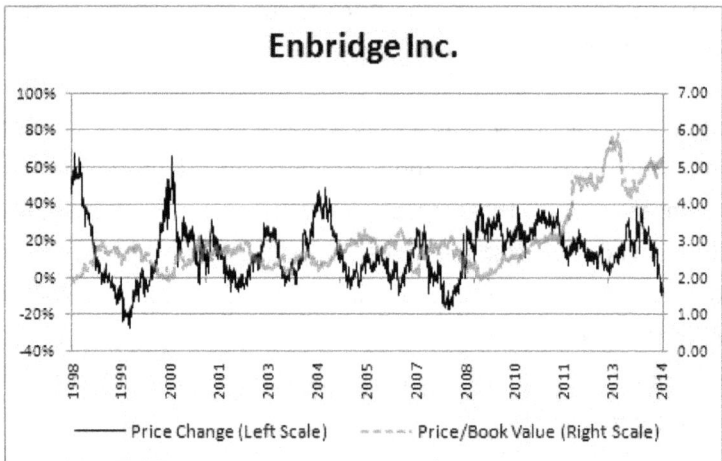

Enbridge Inc.

Price Change (Left Scale)   Price/Book Value (Right Scale)

Enbridge gained 21.2% when the P/BV was equal to or lower than its average, and 11.2% when it was not[8]. Note from the above chart that 1-year price performance goes in almost exactly the opposite direction as Price/Book Value. What better evidence that it can be profitable to buy when P/BV levels are low, and sell when they get too high?

As well, Fortis gained 14.11% on average when the P/BV was at or lower than its average, and just 3.15% when it was above. Sears showed a gain of 3.39% on average at average or higher P/BV and a loss of 4.1% when trading below. Only Loblaws gained more when trading above it's average P/BV; (8.54% compared to 4.81% when trading at or below.)

Our lessons from these several studies must be:

- Price/Book Value is a very important measure to consider when you are looking for a stock in which to invest. It is important though to consider intangible assets – especially goodwill. Goodwill is often shown on companies' balance sheets as an asset long after it has outgrown its worth.

- It is not enough to just buy low P/BV stocks and put your portfolio on auto-pilot. A company's stock price might be down because the company is in trouble, and thus, its P/E and P/BV will be low. P/BV should be viewed in context with other valuation measures (ie: Dividend and Earnings Yields)

Some companies may be among the highest P/BV stocks on the chart for a period of time, only to work their way down to the bottom and back. This not only illustrates why it is important to monitor your portfolio but provides opportunities to move in and out of some positions and ultimately beat the market.

Chapter 11

Putting it All Together

A quick trip to your local library or your favorite book store will yield a myriad of literature about how to invest your money. Some will urge you to track recent price changes and momentum indicators; others will offer you a legion of formulae and ratios to analyse, from ROE analysis to dividend discount, EBITDA and on, and on. Some will encourage you to pick just one metric to watch; say Dividend Yield or P/E, and forget the rest.

I hope that in the past few chapters, I have convinced you that there are three measures in particular that are vital to investment success, and in order to achieve superior returns in the longer term and mitigate the risk from volatile market conditions, you need to pay specific attention to these three barometers. They are, of course, Dividend Yield, Earnings Yield, and Price/Book Value. Now, the challenge is to learn how to use these computations to build and maintain a profitable investment portfolio.

During the period between January 1, 1998, and December 31, 2014, the average dividend yield for all companies that were included in the TSX 60 index in 2014, the average Dividend Yield was 2.49%. The average earnings yield was 5.06%, and the average Price/Book Value was 2.72 times[1].

Collectively, dividends were at their lowest during this period in March of 2006, at 1.6%. Over the following year, the stocks gained 6.4% on average. But in the year after dividends hit their peak of 4.9%, in June 2013, the same stocks gained 26.9%. Kudos to dividend investors!

When average Earnings Yield was at its lowest point of -2.92% in September 1998, investors seemed to pay little heed to the lack of earnings, pushing stocks up 13.25% over the ensuing year. But, when Earnings Yield was at its highest at 14.4% in February 2005, stocks gained 28.3% over the next year – more than double that of the low earnings year and double that of former period.[2]

And even though the Price/Book Value was at its highest, at 3.52 times in March 2006 stocks gained 10.0% over the next 12 months, when Price/Book Value reached its lowest point of 1.71 times in March 2009, investors pushed stock prices up a whopping 57.6% over the next year.[3] There could be no better reinforcement for our assertion that it is better to own/buy stocks when the Price/Book Value is low, and perhaps avoid them when P/BV is high.

It seems then, that the best strategy to maximize investment returns is to seek out companies that have the most favorable combination of high dividend yields, high earnings yields, and low price/book value ratios.

Rounding off the average values above, our first step in selecting individual stocks for your portfolio should be to look for companies whose stocks are trading with a dividend yield of 2.5% or more, an earnings yield of 5.0% or better and are trading at a price not exceeding 2.7 times book value.

The next step requires a computer and access to the internet. We are going to do a search for companies that are currently equal to or better than these numbers. And to do this, you will need to access a stock screener. There are several of these tools on the internet; just Google "stock screener" and take your choice. The following two sites from Google Finance and Yahoo Finance are quite serviceable, and they are free:

Google Finance:
 https://www.google.ca/finance#stockscreener

Yahoo! Finance:
 https://screener.finance.yahoo.com/stocks.html

Here are another two sites, both which charge an annual fee, but provide a wealth of research and data:

Value Line Research: https://jump.valueline.com/login.aspx

Morningstar Research:
 http://www2.morningstar.ca/homepage/h_ca.aspx?culture=e n-CA

Google and Yahoo! Display data going back five years, while Morningstar goes back ten years, and Value Line fifteen. In my humble opinion, the extra data is well worth the few hundred dollars I pay for the premium services.

Pick the stock screener of your choice and start with the average values above. The site will provide several "filters" you can use to enter the criteria you use to choose the stocks you might consider investing in. Key in "Minimum dividend yield": 2.5%; "Minimum Earnings Yield": 5.0% and "Maximum

Price/Book Value": 2.7 times. There will be another filter you can use identified as "Capitalization" or "Market Cap". As an investor who likes to avoid "small-cap" stocks, I key in $1 Billion here.

Using the Google screener, I asked for these criteria for the Canadian market and for all exchanges. Some screeners allow you to combine the Canadian and US markets, but I like to do them separately. To add US stocks just repeat the process, requesting companies from the US instead. The screener gave me a list of 65 stocks from which to choose.

Now we have a list of stocks that represent potential investments, but there are still more than I would want to hold in my portfolio, and we have yet to compare each stock's current metrics to its historical values. This information is available on the same website you used as a screener. Look for stocks that are trading above their own average dividend yield and earnings yield and below their average price/book value. Why that cut-off? Let's review three of the stocks we have covered in past chapters and find out; two of which I would want in my portfolio most of the time and the other - well..... not so much:

TD Bank:

TD Bank paid an average dividend of 3.06% between 1998 and 2014. At times when the dividend matched or exceeded 3.06%, the company's stock gained an average of 14.8% in the ensuing year. When the dividend was less than 3.06%, that capital return was reduced to 8.8%.

TD also reported an average earnings yield of 6.76% between 1998 and 2014. At times when the earnings yield matched or exceeded 6.76%, the company's stock gained an average of 14.9% in the ensuing year. When the earnings yield was less than 6.76%, that capital return was reduced to 7.4%.

And finally, TD traded at an average of 2.06 times book value between 1998 and 2014. At times when the price/book value was equal to or less than 2.06 times, the company's stock gained an average of 14.4% in the ensuing year. When the price/book value was over 2.06 times, that capital return was reduced to 5.20%.

Fortis Inc.

Fortis Inc. paid an average dividend of 3.83% between 1998 and 2014. At times when the dividend matched or exceeded 3.83%, the company's stock gained an average of 10.51 in the ensuing year. When the dividend was less than 3.83%, that capital return was reduced to 7.34%.

Fortis also reported an average earnings yield of 5.92% between 1998 and 2014. At times when the earnings yield matched or exceeded 5.92%, the company's stock gained an average of 18.05% in the ensuing year. When the earnings yield was less than 5.92%, that capital return was reduced to 2.88%.

And finally, Fortis traded at an average of 1.57 times book value between 1998 and 2014. At times when the price/book value was equal to or less than 1.57 times, the company's stock gained an average of 14.11% in the ensuing year. When the price/book value was over 1.57 times, that capital return was reduced to 5.20%.[9]

Sears Canada:

Sears Canada paid an average dividend of 0.34% between 1998 and 2014. At times when the dividend matched or exceeded 0.34%, the company's stock gained an average of 21.06% in the ensuing year. When the dividend was less than 0.34%, that capital return was reduced to a loss of 8.07%.

Note that on several occasions Sears paid special dividends which I have not included in the regular dividend yield.[4] None of these special dividends were part of Sears' ongoing dividend policy, and each came just after the company sold off significant assets. As such, we really can consider them a return of capital – notably to the majority shareholder (Sears in the US). Here is a list of the special dividends:

Table 11-a

Special Dividends	
5/27/2010	$ 3.50
9/20/2010	$ 3.50
12/20/2012	$ 1.00
11/28/2013	$ 5.00
12/9/2013	$ 5.00

Retailing is a very difficult business, and competition is cut-throat. Retail customers can also be extremely fickle. This can result in earnings being quite volatile, and make it difficult to adhere to an unchanging dividend policy. Dividends become unreliable. Sears provides a perfect example of how that can impact investors. No dividends for many years, some dividends in other years, then big pay-outs when the company has sold off assets.

Given this history, one might wonder if there is much value in trying to assign a value to Sears Canada stock based on dividends. For investors who don't mind a lot of stock volatility, and uncertain cash flow (I am not one of those investors), there may be some benefit in buying/holding only when the regular dividend yield in the top two tri-sectors, and selling when it falls below.

Sears Canada also reported an average earnings yield of 9.16% between 1998 and 2014. At times when the dividend matched or exceeded 9.16%, the company's stock gained an average of 10.86% in the ensuing year. When the earnings yield was less than 9.16%, that capital return was turned into a loss of 3.41%.

And finally, Sears Canada traded at an average of 1.81 times book value between 1998 and 2014. At times when the price/book value was equal to or less than 1.81 times, the company's stock gained an average of 3.48% in the ensuing year. When the price/book value was above 1.81 times, that capital became a loss of 3.77%.

So, look for stocks trading at or above their average dividend yield, earnings yield, and below their average price/book value.

Depending on the stock screener you use, you may be able to choose what data are displayed on the screen, and you may be able to export it into MS Excel. From there you can sort the results from high to low for the various yardsticks you have selected. It is important here that you do not just pick the highest combination of yields and price/book value, and buy up the stock.

A mouse click on the company name on any of these screeners will take you to financial data for the company selected. There are more enhanced reports, going back several more years on the Value-Line and Morningstar websites mentioned earlier. Look at that data. Make sure earnings cover the dividend being paid and that the earnings record has been steady and dependable. Remember from our chapter on dividends. If earnings cannot support them, dividends will ultimately be cut.

Another thing to watch for is debt. I have not spent a lot of time setting out debt parameters because various industries typically tend to require different capital structures. Banks and insurance companies may have over 90% of their capitalization in debt. Utilities and pipeline companies are often near 90% as well. Retailers may carry very little debt, depending on whether or not they own their own real estate.

I look for utilities and real estate companies who carry less than 80% debt and manufacturers who carry less than 50% of their capital structure as debt; although some heavy equipment manufacturers like Caterpillar Inc. or John Deere may carry more debt due to the nature of their business. So, when assessing debt, we are not always comparing apples to apples. But when we are, less debt is usually better.

By now you have:

1. gone through the list provided by your stock screener, and selected the better values according to our three metrics,

2. eliminated companies that do not exhibit a record of steady dividend and dividend growth – as well as earnings that can support the dividends

3. filtered out companies trading above their own average values, and

4. made sure you are comfortable with each company's debt profile.

Now you are ready to start buying stocks for your portfolio. Choose those fifteen to twenty stocks with the best combination of yields and price/BV from your list. Try to keep your minimum investment to around $10,000. This will keep a check on transaction costs, and minimize the length of the list of stocks you need to monitor.

When to Sell:

Keep in mind, even once this task has been accomplished – you're not done! Now you have to monitor your portfolio to ensure your investments don't fall outside your acceptable ranges. When should you sell?

Many investment advisors would suggest you "take profits" because a stock has risen 30% since you purchased it – or maybe after it has doubled. Or they may suggest you bail if the stock trades down a certain amount – or perhaps that you "double-down". Don't fall into this trap. <u>Never sell a stock based on its price action alone.</u> Watch the same variables you used to select the stock in the first place, and use them to make your decisions.

All three of our metrics are dynamic in nature. That is they change over time. If your stock has gained 50% in market price, and earnings, book value, and dividends have increased in kind, there is no reason to sell the stock. So, keep an eye on the current values for these metrics.

I don't suggest you buy a stock when it is at its average dividend or earnings yield, then sell it if it dips down to the 49% range – only to buy it back when it hits 50% again. You could be buying and selling the stock every second day. The only one who benefits then is your broker (discount broker or otherwise).

Instead, consider selling when the values dip below 75% of its average for either its earnings or dividend yield and 25% above the average price/book value. So, if the average earnings yield is 10% (your "buy" target), you would set a "sell target" at 7.5%.

This way, you have some cushion, and for most stocks the track record has been good. Let's review those same three stocks from this perspective:

TD Bank:

75% of TD Bank's 3.06% average dividend is 2.30%. At times when the dividend matched or exceeded 2.30%, the company's stock gained an average of 12.60% in the ensuing year. When the dividend was less than 2.30%, that capital return was just 3.10%.

75% of TD's 6.76% average earnings yield is 5.07%. When the earnings yield matched or exceeded 5.07%, the company's stock gained an average of 12.00% in the ensuing year. When the earnings yield was less than 5.07%, that capital return was reduced to 4.20%.

And finally, 125% of TD's average book value of 2.06 times is 2.75 times. When the price/book value was equal to or less than 2.75 times, the company's stock gained an average of 11.90% in the ensuing year. When the price/book value was over 2.06 times, that capital return was reduced to just 2.70%.

Fortis Inc.

75% of Fortis Inc.'s average dividend of 3.83% is 2.87%. At times when the dividend matched or exceeded 2.87%, the company's stock gained an average of 8.76% in the ensuing year. When the dividend was less than 2.87%, that capital return was reduced to 3.09%.

75% of Fortis Inc.'s average earnings yield of 5.92% is 4.44%. At times when the earnings yield matched or exceeded 5.92%, the company's stock gained an average of 9.29% in the ensuing year. Fortis rarely fell below this earnings level, but when the earnings yield was less than 5.92%, that capital return turned into a loss of 12.63%.

And finally, 125% of Fortis Inc.'s average book value of 1.57 times is 2.09. When the price/book value was equal to or less than 2.09 times, the company's stock gained an average of 9.06% in the ensuing year. When the price/book value was over 2.09 times, that capital return was reduced to just 1.68%.

Sears Canada:

75% of Sears Canada's average dividend of 0.34% is 0.26%. At times when the dividend matched or exceeded 0.26%, the company's stock gained an average of 21.05% in the ensuing year. When the dividend was less than 0.26%, that capital return was turned into a loss of 8.08%.

75% of Sears Canada's 9.16% average income yield is 6.87%. At times when the income yield matched or exceeded 6.87%, the company's stock gained an average of 15.97% in the ensuing year. When the earnings yield was less than 6.87%, that capital return was turned into a loss of 8.53%.

And finally, 125% of TD's average book value of 1.81 times book value is 2.41 times. When the price/book value was equal to or less than 2.41 times, the company's stock gained an average of 2.72% in the ensuing year. When the price/book value was above 1.81 times, that capital became a loss of 4.95%.

The above information is shown on the following page in table format: 5

TD Bank	Average:	over	under	75% of Ave	over	under
Div. Yld.	3.06	14.80	8.80	2.30	12.60	3.10
Earn Yld.	6.76	14.90	7.40	5.07	12.00	4.20
Price/BV	2.06	14.40	5.20	2.75	2.70	11.90
Fortis	Average:	over	under	75% of Ave	over	under
Div. Yld.	3.83	10.51	7.34	2.87	8.76	3.09
Earn Yld.	5.92	18.05	2.88	4.44	9.29	(12.63)
Price/BV	1.57	5.20	14.11	2.09	1.68	9.06
Sears	Average:	over	under	75% of Ave	over	under
Div. Yld.	0.34	21.06	(8.07)	0.26	21.05	(8.08)
Earn Yld.	9.16	10.86	3.41	6.87	15.97	(8.53)
Price/BV	1.81	(3.77)	3.48	2.41	(4.95)	2.72

All in all, this data confirms our theory that for the most part, stocks do better when their dividend yields are higher than when they are low. As well, for the most part, stocks do better when their earnings yields are higher than when they are low. And finally, stocks tend to perform better when their price is at a lower multiple to their book value than when the price/book value is higher.

Here is how I put this concept to use: My portfolio is fully invested, and "ABC" stock dips below 75% of its average dividend or earnings yield, or 25% higher than its average price/book value. I check out what's happening with the company. If earnings have just dropped off in a given quarter, but the other two metrics are still strong, I still hold onto the stock and continue to monitor the situation. If a second metric falls below the cut-off, I take another look, and this is when I will probably sell the stock. Unless the company is having significant difficulties and had to cut its dividend, it is likely the stock price has moved up beyond the point where it represents good value. Worry not..... it's a good problem to have. It means you have made money!

Now you've had a few companies trade above their range of good value, you've sold them and you have some cash to reinvest. Simply start the process over again to select new stocks into which to invest. But, as you do so, don't change your benchmarks just because the market has moved up. This may be the most difficult part. If you do your screen, and can't find a quality investment that fits within your benchmarks, put the money into treasury bills, or a good money market mutual fund. This is how your portfolio can time the market for you because if you can't find any stocks trading at or below their average yield and book value ranges, the market is over-priced.

When stock prices in general come back down and revert to their benchmark means, you will have plenty of cash with which to invest. And that is how you beat the market.

Chapter 12

Odds and Ends

Beware the Analyst:

Early in my career as an Investment Advisor I was given a research report; fresh from the printers that was entitled "Sell Imperial Oil - Buy Texaco". I knew I had a long learning curve ahead of me, so I not only delved into the report, but also checked out each company's financial reports to find out why.

To my surprise, the actual earnings trend and other valuation metrics I had been taught in finance class suggested Imperial Oil was in a better position than Texaco. Curious, I took my findings to my branch manager, seeking clarification. I was abruptly told I was to recommend selling Imperial Oil and buying Texaco because that is what "Research" said to do.

Later, I found myself confiding in a friend, who was also in the early stages of his investment career. However, he had been in the business for about four years, and I was just a rookie. Here is what he said "Don't believe everything you read. If an analyst suddenly gets all excited about a stock and starts 'pumping' the thing like that, it might just mean they are in bed with the company, and you can expect an equity issue is coming with us as one of the lead underwriters."

"Wow", I thought. "This guy is a real cynic." Two weeks later Imperial Oil announced a major equity issue was in the works, - and guess who was one of the lead underwriters?

In 2002, then New York State Attorney General Eliot Spitzer took legal action against several major brokerage firms for issuing positive reports about various stocks even when their analysts privately held very negative opinions of the underlying companies - in one case the analyst privately referred to the stock he was promoting publically as "crap". In the end, ten firms (Bear Stearns, Credit Suisse First Boston, Deutsche Bank, Goldman Sachs, J.P. Morgan Chase, Lehman Brothers, Merrill Lynch, Morgan Stanley, Salomon Smith Barney, UBS Warburg) paid a combined $1.4 Billion in fines to settle the case.[1]

About this time, I was curious just how close analysts' earnings estimates were to the real thing. I tracked the International Brokerage Estimate System (I.B.E.S.) average estimate for the S&P 500 from 1974 to 2001 and found that on average, analysts over-estimated earnings collectively by nearly 25%.[2]

US regulators tried to clean up the industry in the early 2000's, passing the Regulation Fair Disclosure (FD) act 2000 and the Sarbanes-Oxley Act (SOX) in 2002.[3] But did it make any difference?

Not according to Washburn University professor Reza Espahbodi, who along with his brother Hassan and sister-in-law Pouran co-authored a paper in 2014 entitled *Did Analyst Forecast Accuracy and Dispersion Improve Following the Increase in Regulation Post 2002?* [4] According to the study, the median forecast error (incorrect earnings projection) increased during the pre-regulation period of 1994–2000, decreased slightly by the end of the short-term post-regulation period of 2003 through 2006, and then increased to back to near pre-regulation levels by the end of the long-term post-regulation period of 2007–2013

In a 2012 report, researchers at the University of Waterloo and Boston College said the credibility and usefulness of target prices has long been dubious, with media and investment managers frequently labeling target prices "as merely sales hype."5 The study included more than 11,000 analysts from 41 countries, the overall accuracy of target prices is not very high, averaging around 18% for a three-month horizon and 30% for a 12month horizon.

So, my advice, when looking at a brokerage research report or considering an analyst's estimate for future earnings is: "Take it with a grain of salt."

Avoiding Leverage:

Dictionary.com defines leverage as "the use of a small initial investment, credit, or borrowed funds to gain a very high return in relation to one's investment, to control a much larger investment, or to reduce one's own liability for any loss." - and if only that were a complete and accurate definition, wouldn't leverage be the answer to all our prayers!

Essentially, leverage is borrowing money, using your own assets as collateral and using the borrowed funds to increase the amount of money you have invested. Let's say you have $50,000 invested in the stock market. You've had some success in the past, and you want to increase your profits. So, you borrow another $50,000 using the assets in your margin account and increase your portfolio to $100,000.

Now, if the market gains 10%, your profits will be 20% instead of 10% on your initial investment. That's $10,000 instead of $5,000 (less interest on the borrowed funds). Here is where reality differs from the simple definition of leverage: We all know the market doesn't always go straight up. If in fact, it goes down 10%, you will have lost $10,000 instead of $5,000, or 20% rather than 10%. And to add insult to injury, your broker is required to demand that you add enough money to your account to bring it back within margin restrictions. Using leverage in this manner does NOT reduce one's liability as suggested above, but rather increases it.

Borrowing in a margin account is not the only way investors increase their leverage (and risk). Buying options, futures contracts, hedge funds or warrants are among several other ways to increase your potential profits as well as multiply your potential losses.

As an example, you can buy a contract which gives you the option to buy 100 shares of a given stock within a certain time period at a certain price. Let's say it is March 25th and you decide to buy 5 option contracts to buy 100 shares per contract (or 500 shares) of Caterpillar (CAT) at $65.00 per share. The contract expires on September 25th. Caterpillar is currently trading at $62.00 per share, and you pay $2.00 for the contract. (That is $2.00 per share or $200 per contract.)

If CAT trades up to $68.00 per share by the time your option expires, you win the difference between $68.00 and the strike price of $65.00 or $3.00 per share. That is a 50% profit. But, if CAT doesn't rise above $65.00 per share by the time the contract expires, you lose your $2.00 per share - or 100% of your investment.

If that doesn't sound risky enough, you could decide to sell option contracts. To do this, you would have to have substantial cash reserves in your investment account just in case you are called upon to buy the stock. Let's say you want to bet against Caterpillar trading above $65.00 per share. You could sell what is called a "naked call" on CAT. In doing this, you collect the $2.00 premium for entering the contract, and if the stock fails to trade above $65.00 by the expiry date, you get to keep the $2.00 and your obligation ends. If however, it does trade above $65.00 you are on the hook for the difference between the share price, and the strike price of your option. What happens if CAT trades all the way up to say..... $87.00 per share? Well, you lose $22.00 per share, less the $2.00 premium you pocket, or $20.00 per share. Yes, using leverage can be quite risky indeed.

Excessive use of leverage led to the stock market crash of 1929 that precipitated the Great Depression - primarily via the use of margin accounts [6]. The 1987 market crash was partly blamed on wholesale sell-offs coinciding with an event known as "triple witching," which describes the circumstances when monthly expirations of options and futures contracts [7] (both examples of leveraged investing) occurred on the same day. In that debacle, the market lost 23% of its value in a single day. In 2001, a bear market was exacerbated by the collapse of several highly levered hedge funds [8]. And in 2008, the world entered what became known as the "Great Recession" after banks and regulators encouraged people to use excessive leverage to borrow against their home equity and then sold those bad mortgages to unwary investors [9].

All in all, leverage may be used efficiently when used in moderation by companies looking to buy new plants and machinery, but I never recommend using leverage in your investment portfolio. Unless you really know what you are doing, the potential gains just don't justify the risk.

Just Say No to the IPO:

An Initial Public Offering (IPO) is the first sale of a company's shares to the public on the open market. Up to that point the company is privately held, and its shares are not available on the stock exchange. Pricing of an IPO is difficult, because there is no observable market price prior to the offering, and because many of the issuing companies have little or no operating history.

Many claim that empirical evidence shows that new IPO's are typically underpriced at issue. They also note that there are hot and cold, markets which exhibit heavy and light volumes. They offer a number of theories to explain the under-pricing. The first is that underwriters may have better information than the issuer about capital markets, so, in order to protect their investment, they convince the issuer to price the issue lower than it might need be. Too much of this tactic may earn them a bad reputation among issuers, however. It was also noted that even investment bankers, who ostensibly are knowledgeable with regard to capital markets under-price their issues too. This suggests there may be some equilibrium level of under-pricing.

Another theory is that there are different levels of investor knowledge. The less informed investor will buy less undervalued issues and more overpriced issues, while the more knowledgeable will buy more of the underpriced issues, but less of the overpriced issues. In order to attract both cohorts, underwriters must under-price on average.

Other theories are that regulators force under-pricing, or that underwriters collude to exploit newer issuers to favour investors. Another suggests that under-pricing is necessary in order to offset risk. Another theory suggests that underpriced new issues leave a "good taste in the investors mouth" so that future underwritings by the same issuer can be sold at a good price.

The problem is, the vast majority of these studies compare the issue price to the market price 30 days hence to draw their conclusions. This leads me to have some serious concern with whether their data reveals true under-pricing of new issues, or rather a systematic "hyping" of IPO's by underwriters and market makers.

Once an IPO is completed, the stock will have market makers, whose function it is to help maintain an orderly market. Invariably the main market maker will be the same firm who was lead underwriter. For all the reasons cited above, it is in the best interest of the underwriter if the new issue is well received in the market, and the price rises above its issue price. In order to appease investors, who the underwriters will wish to sell future issues to, something of a quick profit provides for that "feel good" sensation that might keep investors coming back.

A Little Help From the Underwriters?

As well, I suggest that many underwriters enter the secondary market, in their capacity as market makers, and bid up the price of the newly issued stock to achieve those goals. Is this ethical? No. Is it legal? No way, it is stock manipulation! Is it widespread? I think the evidence I outline below suggests that it is.

A Second Look:

Back in 2002, I listed all of the new stock issues in the first quarter of 2001 on the New York Stock Exchange, and compared the issue price to the closing price at the end of the first day of trading.[10] Then I compared the return in its first complete year with the return of the S&P 500 stock index. I was quite surprised at the first number to develop; that on average, the first-day gains of 8.12% for my sample held for the entire year and the mean return above the S&P 500 for the first 12 months trading was 8.10%.

What stood out, however, was that over half of the positive issues turned into negative returns within the first year, (although they appeared to be offset by one or two spectacular performances). In fact, 12 of the 21 (57.14%) issues provided a lower return at the end of its first 12 months trading than the S&P 500 index. Clearly, even though IPO's may appear to be issued at a premium in the very short term, investors interested in longer-term opportunities should disregard the "hype" that so often accompanies new issues.

From the issuer's perspective, it makes sense to use these short-term phenomena to their advantage. Issue stock when the IPO market is "hot", and when it is not, debt financing may ultimately be cheaper. As well, the issuer should seek out an underwriter who is willing to assume risk by making a firm commitment, and one who has a reputation for "supporting" its new issues.

Now, you might justifiably ask "How relevant is a study performed on the US market in 2002 to the state of the Canadian market today? I asked myself that question, and so I reviewed all IPO's issued and listed on the Toronto Stock Exchange (TSX) in 2013. I compared the issue price for each stock to the market price of that stock on the same day in 2014.[11] I then compared those returns to that of the TSX Composite Index.

There were 39 IPO's issued on the TSX in 2013. Of these 39 stocks, 18 provided positive capital returns, while 21 lost money. The average loss over the year was 1.14%. The average gain for the TSX Index during this period was 14.9%. Seven of the 39 stocks out-performed the TSX Index over the year while 32 of them under-performed the index. Overall, the IPO's from 2013 underperformed the TSX Composite Index by 16.04%.

Bottom line is that if you like to speculate and wish to roll the dice on the quick flip of an IPO, then good luck to you; you'll need it. But if you are a serious investor, looking to stay ahead of the market over the longer term, just say no to the IPO.

Taxes and Your Investments:

Minimizing the taxes you pay is not a part of managing your investments. Maximizing your after-tax returns is. Although I would typically leave detailed analysis to accountants and financial planners, maximizing after-tax returns requires a general understanding and application of Canada's tax laws.

For instance, currently, the top tax rate in Canada for interest income is nearly 50%. The top tax rate for dividends and capital gains, on the other hand, is closer to 30%. Several years ago, when interest rates were higher, and it may have made more sense to keep some of your portfolio in bonds, I would have clients keep their bonds inside their RRSP and their stocks outside their RRSP. Because RRSP income is sheltered until it is drawn out of the account, the overall portfolio attracted less tax.

As well, capital gains are not taxed until the asset in question is sold. Nor are capital losses triggered until sold. This often leads some people to delay transactions they should be making or to make other transactions they should not.

Consider Harvey, who purchased 500 shares of ABC Company four years ago at $20.00 per share. ABC Company has done well, and last year the stock hit $50.00 per share. But times are more difficult of late, and ABC stock no longer fits within Harvey's valuation parameters. It is October, and though the stock is already down to $40.00 on fear ABC Company may have to cut its dividend, Harvey has been advised to hold off selling until January, so as not to trigger a capital gain this year.

This is the worst advice Harvey could possibly get. This stock could very well fall to $20.00 by year-end, and Harvey won't have any capital gains left to worry about. Yet, this kind of advice is doled out with surprising frequency. He should sell the stock and lock in his gains. I was once told: "Never let the tax 'tail' wag the investment 'dog'." Good advice!

Another tricky situation is tax-loss selling. This dilemma may arise late in the year when you have taken a few gains earlier in the same year. You may have a stock or two that have declined in price as a result of overall market conditions, and you are advised to sell those stocks with gains in order to offset your earlier losses, and 'lock in' the current gains for tax purposes.

The problem is, you would like to keep the stocks, as they still represent good value, and in order for the Canadian Revenue Agency (CRA) to recognize the loss, you may not re-purchase the stock for at least 30 days. Should you sell, and hope you can buy them back after 30 days without having to pay more than you sold them for? My advice is to remember the sage advice: "Never let the tax 'tail' wag the investment 'dog'."

This is not a comprehensive review of tax laws applicable to your investments in Canada. Whole books are written about that, and a more detailed discussion does not fall under the purview of this book.

Your tax situation should always be taken into consideration when it affects the after-tax return on your investments, and thus, I felt a brief overview was warranted. Invest in a manner that maximizes not necessarily the amount you earn, but the amount you get to keep. But never twist your investments around to the detriment of returns solely to minimize your taxes.

Don't Buy All at Once:

When Financial Planners talk about 'Dollar Cost Averaging", they are usually referring to systematically buying a set value of mutual funds every month rather than trying to time the market, and plunge your nest egg in all at once. The idea is that you can never time the market and using this strategy although you will indeed be buying when the market is high, you will also be buying when the market is down, and the two extremes will average out. This is not such a bad strategy, and it does work well when you are just starting to build your savings.

But the concept also has merit if you have a more significant amount of cash you wish to put into the market. Fundamentals may suggest a market is undervalued at any given time, but as we established in previous chapters, emotional investors can irrationally push stock prices into extremely over-valued or extremely under-valued levels, and keep them there for significant periods of time. As well, these over/undervalued situations can turn on a dime, with no apparent impetus.

Let's say you just inherited $100,000 and you want to put it into the stock market. You believe the market is currently undervalued, so you buy $100,000 worth of stocks, but irrational investors push the market down another 15% - and you are down $15,000. That's no way to start an investment plan.

But, if instead, you decided to put $35,000 in the market right away, another $35,000 in a month or so, and the final $30,000 in the following month, you will only be down $5,250 after the first tranche, and you are now able to buy more stocks at lower prices. Sure, this strategy eliminates the chances of "getting in at the bottom", but it also eliminates the risk of watching your entire portfolio getting clobbered as soon as you buy it. And the psychological benefit is priceless.

In my closing comments, I would urge you to establish your

plan for investing your portfolio, and stick to it. Set your target ranges for dividend yield, earnings yield, and price/book value (the values I described earlier are pretty good ones.), and keep the process going. Do not fall under the influence of the 'talking heads' who thrive on theatrics, and do not let emotions dictate your investment decisions. Do this, and I'm betting you can beat the market, too.

Notes:

Chapter 1:

1) See: http://www.investopedia.com/terms/r/risk.asp

Chapter 2:

1) PIMCO Investment Management Co. Investment Outlook; August 2002

2) Data Source: Schiller, Robert; Irrational Exuberance, 2nd Edition; Princeton University Press; 2005

3) PIMCO Investment Management Co. Investment Outlook; August 2002

4) Sources: Bureau of Economic Analysis - July 2014 and Statistics Canada May 2014

5) Siegel, Jeremy; Stocks for the Long Run; McGraw Hill; 2014

6) Schiller, Robert; Irrational Exuberance, 2nd Edition; Princeton University Press; 2005

7) Santayana, George; The Life of Reason; Vol.1; 1905

8) Robert; Irrational Exuberance, 2nd Edition; Princeton University Press; 2005

9) Sources: Standard & Poor's Index Services

    Scotia Capital

    Federal Reserve Bank of St; Louis

    Siegel, Jeremy; Stocks for the Long Run; McGraw Hill; 2014

10) Ibid

11) Source: Bank of Canada - Banking & Financial Statistics July 2015

Chapter 3:

1) See: The Obama Administration Bullies GM Bondholders"; Washington Post; May 26, 2009

2) See: The Largest Bankruptcies in American History: The Insider; November 2011

3) Source: Office of the Superintendant of Bankruptcy Canada; CCAA Records List.

4) Source: Bank of Canada

5) Sources: Bank of Canada, Federal Reserve Bank of St. Louis

6) Source: Statistics Canada

7) Source: Bank of Canada

8) Source: Bureau of Economic Analysis

9) Source: Statistics Canada

10) Source: www.economics.about.com

11) Sources: World Gold Council; Kitco Metals Inc.

Chapter 4:

1) McWhinney, J.; A Brief History of the Mutual Fund; Investopedia;2005

2) Ibid

3) Soe, Aye.M.; Standard & Poor's Indexes Vs. Active Funds Scorecard; McGraw Hill Financial; 2013

4) Sources: - The Globe and Mail; Globe Investor; Canadian Mutual Fund Performance Tables - Morningstar Research

5) Ibid

6) Canadian Securities Administrators Staff Notice 33-316 (December 2013)

7) Sources: - The Globe and Mail; Globe Investor; Canadian Mutual Fund Performance Tables

   Morningstar Research

   RBC Canadian Equity Fund Quarterly Report; RBC Global Asset Management; June 2014

8) Chevreau, Jonathan; Shooting the Wounded; The Financial Post; September, 2008

9) Davidson, Lee; The History of Exchange Traded Funds; Morningstar Research; 2012

10) Sources: - The Globe and Mail; Globe Investor; Canadian Mutual Fund Performance Tables 2013

    Morningstar Research

11) Sources: Standard & Poor's S&P/TSX Index Factsheet; 2007 & 2015

12) See: CBC News; Nortel Loses Title as Canada's Biggest Company; August 2001

13) Source: The Accredited Investor Exemption; Ontario Securities Commission

14) Source: www.dictionary.law.com

15: Dealers we Regulate; Investment Industry Regulatory Organization of Canada

16) Online version: www. moneysense.ca

Chapter 5:

1) Chart Source: www.stockcharts.com

2) Chart Source: www.google.ca/finance

3) Fisher, Irving; The Nature of Capital and Income; MacMillan Press; 1906

4) Malkiel, Burton; A Random Walk Down Wall Street; W.W.Norton & Co.; 1973

5) Fama, Eugene; Foundations of Finance: Portfolio Decisions and Securities Prices; Basic Books; 1976

6) Sharp, William; Portfolio Theory and Capital Markets; McGraw Hill; 1970

7) Fama, Eugene & Miller, Merton; The Theory of Finance; Holt, Rinehart & Winston; 1972

8) As quoted in "The Politics of Public Funding: How to Modify Wall Street to Fit Main Street" by Ben Finkelstein; 2006

Chapter 6:

1) Paul Samuelson was a Nobel Laureate and Professor of Economics at M.I.T. as well as being consultant to several US presidents.

2) Sources: Scotia Capital, Toronto Stock Exchange, C.D. Howe Institute (Turning Points: Business Cycles in Canada since 1926; October 2012)

3) Financial Post 2008

4) Mlambo, Lyman; Adaptive and Rational Expectations Hypothesis; Reviewing the Critiques; Journal of Economic Behaviour; 2012

5) Bignell, William; The Good, the Bad and the Ugly; Leon Frazer & Associates; 2004

6) Krugman, Paul; Running out of Bubbles; New York Times; May, 2005

7) During a debate on Fox News Peter Schiff came under intense criticism when he commented: "The US economy is not strong and the housing market will crash, and we will have high unemployment."

8) Source: American Bankruptcy Institute

9) In December 1996, Alan Greenspan (then Governor of the US Federal Reserve) offered the opinion that "irrational exuberance may have unduly escalated asset values" and

questioned if they "might become subject to a prolonged contraction as they had in Japan."

10) Greenspan, Alan; I Never Saw it Coming" Foreign Affairs; September 2013

11) Greenspan, Alan; The Map and the Territory: Risk, Human Nature and the Future of Forecasting; Penguin Press; 2013

12) Keynes, John Maynard; The General Theory of Employment Interest and Money; Palgrave, MacMillan; 1936

13) Buffett made this statement in an interview on PBS with Charlie Rose on October 1, 2008

14) There are several formulae to determine Present Value, depending on what type of receipts are being measured; be they a series of bond coupons or a single payment. In its simplest form, assume you are contracted to receive $100.00 in one years' time, and the current interest rate is 5.0%. The present value of this contract is: $P/V = FV/(1+r) = 100/(1+.05) = 95.238.

15) Source: Investopedia.com

Chapter 7:

1) Lynch, Peter; Beating the Street; Simon & Schuster Paperbacks; 1993

2) Bigda, Carolyn; The Worst Investments Warren Buffett Ever Made; Kiplingers Personal; 2015

3) Elton, E.J.; Gruber, M.J.; Risk Reduction and Portfolio Size; Journal of Business; 1977

4) Source: Bank of Canada, Statistics Canada

5) Ibid

6) Source: Toronto Stock Exchange

7) Source: www.google.ca/finance

8) Sources: Harvard University; Top 20 Nations Listed by Stock Market Capitalization;2013 - World Bank; Market Capitalization of Listed Companies

9) Source: Morgan Stanley: MSCI Inc.

10) Source: General Electric Co. 2014 Annual Report

11) Source: Exxon 2014 Annual Report

12) Source: Suncor Ltd. 2014 Annual Report

13) Source: Magna International Ltd. 2014 Annual Report

14) Source: Total Petroleum 2014 Annual Report
15) Source: Toyota Motor Co. 2014 Annual Report
16) Source: Honda Motor Co. 2014 Annual Report
17) Source: Anhueser Bush 2014 Annual Report
18) Source: Canon Inc. 2014 Annual Report
19) Source: Sony International Inc. 2014 Annual Report
20) Source: Unilever International Inc. 2014 Annual Report
21) See: "Understanding American Depository Receipts" on the Fidelity Wealth Management website.

Chapter 8:
1) Miller, M. and Modigliani, F; Dividend Policy, Growth and the Valuation of Shares; Journal of Business; 1961
2) Sources: Scotia Capital, National Bank Financial, Statistics Canada
3) Sources: Financial Post Data Services, Enbridge annual reports
4) Ibid
5) Sources: Financial Post Data Services, Fortis Inc. annual reports
6) Ibid
7) Sources: Financial Post Data Services, TD Bank annual reports
8) Ibid
9) Source: Financial Post Data Services
10) Ibid
11) Ibid
12) Ibid
13) Ibid
14) Sources: Financial Post Data Services, Loblaw Companies annual reports
15) Ibid
16) Source Financial Post Data Services, Sears Canada Annual Reports
17) Ibid
18) Name withheld - This T-V show was televised nationally.
19) The stock had traded down from $42.00 US. It has never recovered.

20) Source: Value Line Investor Services

21) Again, this opinion was televised on National T-V.

22) The Canadian government has since increased the Tier 1 Capital Ratio requirement to 8.5%

23) Sources: Financial Post Data Services, National Bank annual reports

Chapter 9:

1) Graham, Ben & Dodd, David; Securities Analysis; McGraw Hill Books; 1934 - This book has been revised several times. The 6th edition is now in print.

2) Nicholson, S. Francis; Price/Earnings Ratios; Financial Analysts Journal; 1960

3) McWilliams, James D.; Prices and P/E Ratios; Financial Analysts Journal; 1966

4) Miller, Paul & Widmann, Ernst; Price Performance Outlook for high and Low P/E Stocks; Commercial & Financial Chronicle; 1966

5) Breen, William; Low Price-Earnings and Industry Relatives; Financial Analysts Journal; 1966

6) Breen, William & Savage, James; Portfolio Distribution and Tests of Security Selection Models; Journal of Finance; 1968

7) Fama, Eugene & French, Kenneth; The CAPM is Wanted, Dead or Alive; Journal of Finance; 1966

8) Graham, Benjamin; The Intelligent Investor; Harper Row Publishers; 1973

9) Dremman, David; Contrarian Investment Strategies; Simon & Schuster; 2012

10) Siegel, Jeremy; Stocks for the Long Run - 5th Edition; McGraw Hill; 2014

11) Source: Historical Components of the Dow Jones Industrial Average; Wikipedia.org

12) Source: Netinvestor.org

13) Reuters News; Timeline: Most Impactful Events of the US Financial Crisis; 2012

14) Source: Fiderer, David; The CDO's that Destroyed AIG; Huffington Post; May, 2010

15) Source: American Bankruptcy Institute

16) Reuters News; Timeline: Most Impactful Events of the US Financial Crisis; 2012

17) Source: Value Line Investor Services

18) Data Source: Schiller, Robert; Irrational Exuberance; Princeton University Press; 2009

19) Ibid

20) Source: Financial Post data Services, Enbridge annual reports; http://ca.finance.yahoo.com

21) Source: Financial Post data Services, Loblaw Companies annual reports; http://ca.finance.yahoo.com

Chapter 10:

1) Source: Value Line Investor Services

2) Ibid

3) Ibid

4) Sources: Gillette annual reports & Proctor & Gamble annual reports

5) Ibbotson, Robert; Decile Portfolios of the New York Stock Exchange 1967 - 1984; Yale School of Management; 1986

6) Dremman, David; Contrarian Investment Strategies; Simon & Schuster; 2012

7) Dow constituents provided by Wikipedia. Stock prices provided by Yahoo/finance.com

Chapter 11:

1) Data Sources: SEDAR (System for Electronic Document Analysis & Retrieval). www.wikinvest.com; Yahoo.finance.ca, company annual and quarterly reports

2) Ibid

3) Ibid

4) Sears Canada corporate reports

5) Data Sources: SEDAR (System for Electronic Document Analysis & Retrieval). www.wikinvest.com; Yahoo.finance.ca, company annual and quarterly reports

Chapter 12:

1) Source: The Economist; Consistently Wrong; January 2014

2) Data Source: International Brokerage Estimate System (IBES); Thomson Financial; Robert Schiller - Irrational Exuberance

3) See: Analyst Crackdown Did Nothing to Improve US Earnings Forecasts; Bloomberg Business; June 2015

4) Hassan and Pouran Espahbod are Professors of Business at University of Texas. Reza Espahbod is a Professor of Accounting at Washburn University.

5) Alan Huang & Hongping Tan (University of Waterloo) and Mark Bradshaw (Boston College); Analyst Target Prices and Forecasting Accuracy around the World; April 2012

6) Colombo, Jessie; Black Monday: The Stock Market Crash of 1929; The Bubble Bubble; July 2012

7) Colombo, Jessie; Black Monday: The Stock Market Crash of 1987; The Bubble Bubble; July 2012

8) Colombo, Jessie; The Dot Com Bubble; The Bubble Bubble; 2012

9) See: Crash Course; The Economist; 2013

10) The New York Stock Exchange provides ongoing information about all companies listing on their exchange. The website is at: www,nyse.com

11) Similarly, the Toronto Stock Exchange(TSX) provides data on all new issues. The TSX web site is at: www.tmx.com

Glossary of Terms

1987 Market Crash: On October 19, 1987, the stock market, along with the associated futures and options markets, crashed, with the S&P 500 stock market index falling over 20 percent. Canada's TSE 300 Index (the precursor to the S&P TSX Composite Index) fell about 23%. Markets had reached "bubble" proportions on the back of excessive leveraging and general euphoria. Concern about a rising US trade deficit and rising interest rates caused a reversal of recent market gains, and high volume triggered massive computerized trading programs that served to exacerbate an already falling market.

Accelerated Capital Depreciation: When companies make large capital expenditures, they write off the cost over several years against their income tax, in order to match ongoing income with the lifetime of the asset. In order to encourage investment, governments may allow them to write these assets of at a faster pace, in order to reduce current taxes.

Adaptive Expectations: An economic theory that assumes that current conditions influence peoples' expectations for future conditions. For example, interest rates have been very low for many years now, and because of this, most people expect interest rates to remain low for the foreseeable future.

American Depositary Receipt (ADR): An ADR is a negotiable certificate issued by an American bank confirming that the bank is holding a specified number of shares in a foreign corporation for each ADR. The bank looks after converting share prices, dividends etc. into American dollars.

Asian Contagion: In 1997, a financial crisis in Thailand resulted in the country dramatically devaluing its currency, and losing all confidence of foreign investors. This situation spread to other Southeast Asian countries--including Malaysia, Indonesia and the Philippines. The end result was not only the implosion of most Far-Eastern currencies, but a subsequent bailout by the International Monetary Fund, and a severe contraction of global equity markets.

Balance of Payments: The measure of all payments in and out of a country. This includes imports/exports (the current account) as well as interest and dividends (the capital account).

Bank Capitalization Rates (Cap Rates): In order to ensure commercial banks are always able to meet the demands of depositors when they want to make cash withdrawals from their accounts, they keep a certain percentage of their overall capital in cash. Prior to the financial crisis of 2008, most countries required their banks to hold at least 5.0% in reserves. At the time, Canada's "Big- six" all held reserves in the 10% range, earning Canada's banking system the reputation as the world's safest Required reserves have been increased to 7.0% in most jurisdictions, and many expect it to continue to increase.

Bank of Canada: The Bank of Canada is Canada's central bank. A central bank is an entity charged with the responsibility of overseeing the country's monetary system, and is responsible for setting short-term interest rates and administering the country's supply of money. In turn, the Bank is partially responsible for affecting inflation and unemployment, as well as bearing some responsibility for regulating and supervising

Canada's commercial banks.

Bear Market: A bear market is any market (stocks, bonds, real estate) that is in an elongated downward trend. A stock market is generally considered to be in "bear" territory after it has declined 20% or more from its high point.

Behavioral Economics: Traditional economists forecast markets and economies using supply and demand-like charts and an array of intricate mathematical formulae. Their result usually gives them a reasonable expectation of where things should be, assuming they are "in balance" and all market participants always act rationally. Unfortunately, however, things are usually not in balance, and forecasts are wrong more often than they are right. Behavioral economics introduces psychology into the equation, and tries to determine why markets are "out of balance" and what makes people behave in ways that would push an economy or market above or below that balanced position.

Bimetallic Currency System: Throughout the middle ages, the Renaissance and into the 20th century, much of the world's economies operated on a bimetallic currency system, where all money was backed by a fixed level of gold or silver. Early in the 20th century, most economies replaced their bimetallic system with "Fiat Currency" which means the currency is backed by the "good faith" of the government in charge.

Blue Chip: A blue-chip stock is common equity in a high quality, long-standing company that has, and is expected to continue to thrive in both good times and bad.

Bonds: A bond is a contractual promise to pay the bond holder an agreed upon amount of cash at a given date. Usually there is also an agreement that the issuer will pay a predetermined interest payment at certain intervals. Bonds may be issued by governments or corporations. Holders of corporate bonds have no voting rights at company meetings, but they do stand in line ahead of stock holders for payment in the event of dissolution of the company.

Book Value Per Share (BVPS): Most companies include the book value per share in their financial statements, and if they don't it is not a difficult ratio to calculate. A balance sheet starts out by listing all assets, then subtracts liabilities – as well as the value of preferred shares, and comes up with a value of equity "attributable to common shares". Let's say that value is $100 million. If the company has 10 million shares outstanding, its book value per share is $10.00.

Bubble: A bubble is a condition that exists when market speculation and irrational euphoria causes participants push prices well above their intrinsic value. Behavioral finance theory attributes stock market bubbles to cognitive biases that lead to groupthink and herd behavior. History is strife with incidents of market bubbles, dating back to the 1600's with Tulipmania and the South-Sea Bubble to more recent instances such as the Dot.Com stock market bubble in 2001 and the Real-Estate bubble in 2008.

Bull Market: A bull market is said to be underway when the market for a given asset class (stocks, bonds, gold, real estate) is on a sustained, long-term incline. One common measure says that a bull market exists when at least 80% of all stock prices rise over an extended period.

Capital Appreciation: (AKA Capital Gain) Capital gains may be realized or unrealized. An unrealized capital gain is calculated as the difference between the current market price of a stock you hold compared to the price you paid for it, times the number of shares you hold (assuming they are currently higher than they were when you bought them). A realized capital gain is the price you sold them for minus the price you paid, times the number shares involved. These numbers should be adjusted for transaction & carrying costs. A capital loss is the reverse condition.

Cash Flow: Like earnings, cash flow per share is a favorite measure of value to many analysts. The difference between cash flow and reported earnings is that the reported earnings number is calculated after recognizing the amortization of goodwill and other non-tangible assets, and the depreciation of tangible assets. Cash flow is considered even more important than reported income to many analysts because it shows us the actual funds that are available to a company for operations.

Cash or Equivalent: Portfolio statements usually have a section that lists the kind of assets (stocks, bonds etc.) that are held. Cash and Equivalents includes all cash holdings, as well as any liquid assets that mature within one calendar year.

Certified Financial Planner (CFP): In Canada, there are no restrictions on one calling him/herself a financial planner. One only needs to take a short course on mutual funds, get licensed, call him/herself a financial planner and he/she is in business. A Certified Financial Planner however, is a designation awarded by the Financial Planners Standards Council after a person successfully completes a series of comprehensive courses relating to investing, insurance, taxes and estate planning. Even after qualifying, a CFP must take continuing educational courses in order to maintain their certification.

Collateralized Debt Obligation (CDO): A CDO is a security in which a collection of assets, usually mortgages, car loans or even credit card debt is pooled together, and sold to individual investors in similar format as a mutual fund.

Common Stock: Common stocks are shares in the equity of a company (hence the word equities or common shares often being used in its place). They are its owners. Common shareholders usually get to vote at annual meetings and choose the directors of the company. It usually takes a major shareholder, however, to have any real influence. Common shareholders are entitled to all earnings of the company, after creditors and preferred shareholders are paid, although companies are not allowed to pay out dividends to common shareholders as they are to preferred shareholders. Common shareholders stand behind all creditors, bondholders and preferred shareholders in the event of dissolution of the company.

Contraction: A contraction can relate to a given market (stock/bond) or to the economy as a whole. It simply means the entity has gotten smaller. A market that has declined for several days or weeks has contracted, but it may not yet be serious enough to be considered a correction (usually considered to be 10%) or a bear market. All corrections and bear markets are contractions, but not all contractions are bear markets or even corrections. Similarly, the economy may contract for two or three months, but still avoid recession. Usually two consecutive calendar quarters of contraction are required to consider an economy to be in recession.

Contrarian: A contrarian is someone who generally believes the opposite of the consensus. If you believe it is possible to get a leg up on other investors by analyzing market or company fundamentals, many analysts would consider you a contrarian. A true contrarian however, believes the consensus is always wrong, and so the only way to beat the market is to observe what every-one else is doing, and just do the opposite.

Correction: A market that has contracted by 10% is considered to be in a correction.

Correlation: Correlation measures the relationship between two variables (say the TSX returns and bond returns). If the two variables are "perfectly positively related" they will have a covariance of 1.0 - which really means their performance is identical. At the other extreme, correlation could be as low as -1.0, which means the variables are "perfectly negatively correlated", and when one variable goes up 8%, the other always goes down 8% etc. A situation where two variables have no relationship at all would have a correlation of zero.

Debt/Service Ratio: Companies and people have debt/service ratios. This is the cost of carrying your debt as a percentage of your net income Economists keep an eye on the collective debt/service ratio for all consumers, which is tracked by

Statistics Canada in Canada and the Bureau of Economic Analysis in the US.

Default Risk: This is the risk that a bond issuer is at some time unable to meet interest payments as stipulated in the terms of the bond issue, or that it may be unable to redeem the face value of the bond at maturity.

Defensive: Defensive stocks are equities that, while they may not generate prolific gains when the market is on the rise, they tend to hold their value when the market is falling. Portfolios can be considered defensive if most of the stocks held are of this nature, or if it has a high proportion of cash and short-term securities.

Deferred Sales Charge: The deferred sales charge is a penalty for "early" redemption that starts out at a certain percentage, and gradually declines until it reaches zero at the end of the specified term. For instance, it may be 5% if the fund is cashed out in the first year, 4% in the second, 3% in the third, and so on.

Deficit: Current Account: This is a situation when a country's imports exceed its exports.

Deficit: Fiscal: A Fiscal deficit it a situation where the government spends more money than it brings in from taxes.

Depression: An economic depression is a severe and long-term contraction of an economy. It is more severe than a recession.

Discount Broker: A discount broker provides access to markets as well as various levels of research. Generally, they do not provide advice about structuring your portfolio or which stocks to buy, and their commissions are significantly lower than full-service brokers.

Discretionary Investment Management: Discretionary Investment Management is the delegation of the day-to-day management of your investments to a professional Investment Counsellor/Portfolio Manager (IC/PM).

Diversification: Portfolio risk is partly managed by spreading one's investments among several stocks – not putting all your eggs in one basket. Statistics show that much of a portfolio's risk is mitigated by holding at least ten issues. Most non-market risk is eliminated with 20 or more stocks. You can also diversify geographically, between different industry sectors, and of course, asset classes.

Dividends: A dividend is a sum of money paid out by a company to its shareholders. The amount per share is generally decided upon by the company's board of directors.

Dividend Irrelevance Theory: A theory, developed by Franco Modigliani and Merton Miller. Basically it is a long mathematical argument that claims that neither the price of firm's stock nor its cost of capital are affected by its dividend policy. In other words, investors should not care whether a company pays dividends or not.

Dividend Policy: A company's dividend policy is the set of guidelines a company uses to decide how much of its earnings it will pay out to shareholders. Many companies target a certain percentage of their earnings to be paid out in dividends.

Dow Jones Industrial Average (DJIA): The DJIA consists of thirty of the largest industrial corporations in the US. It was devised by financial reporters Charles Dow and Edward Jones in 1896 to provide a general view of how the overall market for stocks was faring on any given day. Each stock within the index is weighted according to that company's market capitalization. The DJIA remains a bellwether measuring stick to this day.

Earnings Yield: Earnings per share divided by a stock's price (E/P): The inverse of P/E (the price/earnings ratio).

Economic Indicators: These are statistical measurements or conditions used by analysts and economists to measure economic activity. Examples of economic indicators would be the unemployment rate, retail sales, the consumer confidence index and so on.

Economic Contraction: An economic contraction may be part of a recession, but not necessarily so. Recessions are generally two or more calendar quarters long. A contraction may just consist of one or two months of declining economic activity.

Economic Recession: In Canada, Statistics Canada declares when the country has slipped into recession. The Bureau of Economic Analysis does the job in the US. As a rule of thumb, most analysts consider two consecutive calendar quarters of declining economic activity (GDP) a recession.

Economic Recovery: This is the period when GDP has stopped declining, and started growing again, but it has not yet risen to the level it was at before the recession.

Economic Expansion: This is when the economy has returned to level of activity prior to a recession, and it continues to expand.

Efficient Markets Theory (EMT): EMT is a theory about financial markets that is based on the belief that the dissemination of information relating to capital markets is so efficient, that securities prices always reflect all public and private information there is to know about a company. Thus, no matter how good you are, or no matter how much research you do, you cannot beat the market.

Equities: Common stocks in a company represents the equity shareholders own in that company. Thus, the term equities is often used interchangeably with the term common stocks.

Equity Risk Premium: Equity risk premium is also referred to as simply equity premium. It is the return that investing in the stock market provides in excess of government treasury bonds. It represents the return required to compensate investors for taking on the relatively higher risk of equity investing.

Exchange Traded Funds (EFT): An exchange traded fund, is a marketable security that tracks an index, a commodity, bonds, or a basket of assets like an index fund. Unlike mutual funds, an ETF trades like a common stock on a stock exchange.

Federal Reserve Board (The Fed): The Federal Reserve Board the central bank for the USA. A central bank is an entity charged with the responsibility of overseeing the country's monetary system, and is responsible for setting short-term interest rates and administering the country's supply of money. The Fed influences the overall economy through its control over interest rates and the supply of money.

Fiat Money: Fiat money is currency that is not backed by gold, but rather by the "full faith and credit" of the issuing government. It is accepted as money because a government says that it's legal tender, and the public has enough confidence and faith in the money's ability to serve as a storage medium for purchasing power.

Fiduciary Duty: A fiduciary duty is a legal duty to act solely in another party's interests. Parties owing this duty are called fiduciaries. The individuals to whom they owe a duty are called principals. A fiduciary duty is the highest standard of care entrusted to investment professionals.

Fiscal Policy: Fiscal Policy is the use by governments of taxes and spending in order to influence the economy. By increasing their spending, governments hope to create demand for goods and services, thus increasing overall economic activity.

Fiscal Position: This refers to whether the government is running a surplus or a deficit in its overall budget.

Fundamental Analysis: The fundamentals of a company includes items found in its financial statements. Reviewing these reports, one can determine earnings trends, debt ratios, book value of a company and numerous other metrics. Using these metrics to evaluate a company is referred to as fundamental analysis.

Generally Accepted Accounting Practices (GAAP): When performing fundamental analysis of a company, analysts must be able to compare the metrics of one company to others. The only way the analyst can be sure he/she is comparing apples to apples is if all public companies are required to prepare their financial statements in the same manner.

Government Treasury Bills (T-Bills): Like government bonds, T-bills are debt instruments issued by government entities that promise to pay the holder a sum of money at maturity. Unlike bonds, T-Bills do not come with interest coupons. Rather, T-Bills are issued at a discount to their face (maturity) value, and the difference between the selling price and the maturity value is the implied interest rate. Treasury Bills are issued for a term of one year or less.

Gross Domestic Product (GDP): GDP is the total value of economic activity within an economy over the course of a given time frame – adjusted for imports and exports. GDP consists of all revenues generated by: Government, Investment and Consumers and is adjusted by net exports. It is calculated monthly, quarterly and annually. The most closely watched number is year over year GDP growth; expressed in percentage points. GDP growth adjusted for inflation is referred to as Real GDP Growth.

Growth Stocks: Growth stocks may or may not pay dividends. Investors in growth stocks are primarily looking for capital gains. They tend to be more risky and volatile than more conservative, income stocks.

Hedge Fund: A Hedge Fund is a pool of capital that invests in a variety of different strategies. They are usually structured so that the fund managers can take long and short positions in order to exploit both up and down markets. A transaction for a long position is one whereby the investor buys a stock or bond etc. and pays for it.

Income Stocks: Income stocks could be either high dividend-paying common stocks or preferred shares, which are a hybrid security having some characteristics of common stocks and some characteristics of bonds. Preferred shares technically represent equity in a firm, and therefore income payments qualify as dividends rather than interest. This is important for tax considerations. Although companies are not contractually obligated to pay preferred dividends like they are obligated to pay bond interest, companies may not pay dividends on their common shares if preferred share dividends are in arrears.

Inflation: A sustained increase in the general price of goods and services, inflation is measured by the Consumer Price Index (CPI).

Initial Public Offering (IPO): An Initial Public Offering (IPO) is the first sale of a company's shares to the public on the open market. Up to that point the company is privately held, and its shares are not available on the stock exchange.

Intangible Assets: An intangible asset is an asset that is not physical in nature. Items such as patents, trademarks, copyrights, business methodologies), goodwill and brand recognition are all common intangible assets. How a company accounts for inventory depletion or recognized the value of intangible assets such as goodwill can have a significant impact on its book value and earnings.

Interest Rate Risk: Interest rate risk is the risk that market interest rates may go up after you purchased a bond. This tends to devalue the cash-flow you receive and reduce the market value of your bond.

International Accounting Standards Board (IASB): The IASB is the independent standard-setting body of the IFRS Foundation responsible for the development and publication of IFRSs and for approving Interpretations of IFRSs as developed by the IFRS Interpretations Committee

International Financial Reporting Standards (IFRS): The International Financial Reporting Standards are designed as a common global language for business affairs so that company accounts are understandable and comparable across international boundaries.

Intrinsic Value: Intrinsic value refers to the value of a company, stock, currency or product which is determined through fundamental analysis without reference to its market value.

Investing: To invest is to put up money or another asset with the realistic expectation of generating future income or capital appreciation.

Investment Industry Regulatory Organization of Canada (IIROC): IIROC is the national self-regulatory organization which oversees all investment dealers and trading activity on debt and equity marketplaces in Canada.

Labour Productivity: Labour productivity is defined by Statistics Canada as real gross domestic product (GDP) per hour worked.

Leveraging: To leverage is to borrow money, using your own assets as collateral and using the borrowed funds to increase the amount of money you have invested. Leveraging increases the potential rewards of investing, but it also increases potential losses. Leveraging can be accomplished by borrowing from an external source (ie: bank loans), by using a margin account at your brokerage house or by purchasing certain financial instruments such as options, financial futures hedge funds etc.

Liquidity: Liquidity refers to the ease with which an asset can be converted to cash. The more liquid an asset is, the more liquid it is. Bank term deposits, government treasury bills and money-market mutual funds are most liquid, and are considered to be equal to cash.

Load Fees: A load fee is a sales charge or commission which is paid to a mutual fund company (to be shared with the salesperson) by the purchaser for the privilege of investing in the fund. Mutual fund sales people are required to inform the investor at the time of sale what kind of load is being assessed, and how much it is. Load fees can be paid as front-end (at the time of purchase), back-end (when the fund is redeemed) or as a deferred sales charge. A deferred sales charge is a back-end load which remains higher for the first few years you hold a fund, then gradually starts to decline annually until it finally reaches zero.

M1: The money supply for a given county is categorized according to liquidity. M1 is the narrowest definition of money in Canada and consists of all currency (bills and coins) as well as chequing account deposits.

M2: M2 is the next most liquid monetary definition after M1, and includes M1 + personal savings deposits + non-personal notice deposits.

Management Expense Ratio (MER): The Management Expense Ratio refers to a fee charged by a mutual fund company directly to the mutual fund. The fund company is required to disclose the MER to investors, but it is usually found buried deep within the fund prospectus. The MER includes management fees paid to the fund managers as well as any commissions, accounting, and other expenses. It can range from just over 1% on fixed income funds to well over 3% on many active equity funds or asset allocation funds. The average MER for actively managed equity funds seems to be around 2.5%.

Market Anomalies: Any phenomenon that does not fit within the expectations of Efficient Markets Theory is considered a market anomaly. This would include the P/E Effect and the tendency for high-dividend stocks to out-perform the market over time.

Market Recovery: This is the period when market has stopped declining, and started increasing again, but it has not yet risen to the level it was at before the bear market ensued.

Mexican Currency Crisis: After several decades of strong economic growth, buoyed by high oil prices, the Mexican economy struggled in the 1980's and into the 1990's. The Mexican treasury began issuing short-term debt instruments denominated in domestic currency with a guaranteed repayment in U.S. dollars, attracting foreign investors. In 1994 the Mexican government devalued the peso against the US dollar, causing confidence of investor confidence in the ability of Mexico to meet its obligations, a flight of capital from Mexico, and near-bankruptcy of the Mexican government.

Modern Portfolio Theory (MPT): Modern Portfolio Theory embraces the concept of efficient markets. It concludes that if it is impossible to beat the market, then the only way to increase one's return is to leverage his/her portfolio by borrowing.

Momentum Stocks: Momentum "investors" (I consider them speculators) try to reap high returns by purchasing stocks that are already increasing in price and selling, or perhaps short-selling stocks when they have already established a downward trend.

Monetary Policy: Monetary Policy is a tool used by central banks in order to influence economic activity in hopes to affect unemployment and/or inflation. It is the central bank that controls the supply of money and short-term interest rates in an economy. If the central bank hopes to reduce unemployment, it may reduce short-term interest rates and increase the supply of money. If it is concerned over increasing inflation, it may reduce the money supply and increase interest rates.

Money Market Fund (MMF): A Money Market Fund is a

mutual fund that invest only in debt instruments that mature within a one-year time frame. This may include bank term deposits, short-term corporate instruments or government treasury bills.

Money Supply: Money supply is the entire stock of monetary assets within an economy. This would include money held in cash & chequing accounts (M1), personal savings deposits + non-personal notice deposits (when added to M1, this constitutes M2) as well as money market funds and other short-term instruments (when added to M2, this constitutes M3).

Mortgage Backed Security (MBS): An MBS is a mutual-fund like asset that is backed by a group or collection of mortgages.

Mutual Funds: A mutual fund is a pool of assets set up in a trust, which is funded by a variety of investors, and comprised of stocks, bonds, treasury bills or other securities, or a combination of these assets; or perhaps even other mutual funds.

Organization of Petroleum Exporting Countries (OPEC): OPEC is an international group of thirteen oil exporting countries, founded in the early 1960's. Its stated mission is: "to coordinate and unify the petroleum policies of its member countries and ensure the stabilization of oil markets, in order to secure an efficient, economic and regular supply of petroleum to consumers, a steady income to producers, and a fair return on capital for those investing in the petroleum industry."

P/E Effect: The P/E Effect is the phenomenon, proved by several studies concluding that low P/E stocks outperform high P/E stocks by a large margin.

P/E Ratio: The P/E ratio is the market price of a stock divided by its most recent 12-months earnings per share.

Pooled Fund: A Pooled Fund is similar to a mutual fund, however it is generally a proprietary product offered by a financial institution for use by their in-house customers.

Portfolio: A group of financial assets such as stocks, bonds, notes or other instruments held by any entity. It could be an individual portfolio, held by a private investor, or a much larger portfolio held by a mutual fund, financial institution or pension fund.

Preferred Shares: Preferred shares are a hybrid security with many of the characteristics of common shares, yet several characteristics of bonds, and line up in between bondholders and common shareholders in the event of dissolution of the company. While common shareholders are entitled to all earnings of the company, after creditors and preferred shareholders are paid, companies are not allowed to pay out dividends to common shareholders as they are to preferred shareholders.

Present Value: There are several formulae to determine Present Value, depending on what type of receipts are being measured; be they a series of bond coupons or a single payment. In its simplest form, assume you are contracted to receive $100.00 in one years' time, and the current interest rate is 5.0%. The present value of this contract is:

$P/V = FV/(1+r) = 100/(1+.05) = \$95.238.$

Price to Book Value (P/BV): Book value of a company is calculated by listing all assets, then subtracts liabilities – as well as the value of preferred shares, and comes up with a value of equity "attributable to common shares". Book value per share is this number divided by the number of common shares outstanding. Price to book value is simply the market price of the company's common stock divided by its book value per share.

Price to Earnings (P/E Ratio): Price to Earnings is simply the market price of a company's common stock divided by its most recent twelve-months earnings per share. Forward P/E ratios are also calculated by analysts using the current market price divided by estimated future earnings.

Principal Protected Note: A Principal Protected Note (PPN) is similar to a segregated fund, in that it guarantees your principal will be returned at the end of a certain time frame. Terms range up to 10 years. Typically PPN's are tied to a certain equity market such as the S&P/TSX Composite Index, and they pay investors a percentage of that market returns. Some PPN's pay out up to 75% of the market return, but I have seen somewhere the payout is maxed at as low as 25%.

Quantitative Easing (QE): Quantitative Easing is a monetary tool of central banks which is rarely used. It involves the bank entering the open market, and purchasing longer term government bonds, and simultaneously printing cash and/or short-term securities. The effect of this action is to lower interest rates and to encourage consumers to boost spending, as a strategy to generate economic growth. The strategy also tends to drive down the local currency, boosting exports and curtailing exports.

Quick Ratio: Two of the easiest things to find on a company's balance sheet are its current assets and its current liabilities The quick ratio (also known as the acid test) is simply the current assets divided by the current liabilities.

Rational Expectations: Rational Expectations is an economic argument that presumes economic and market participants take fundamental realities into consideration when making economic decisions.

Real Estate Investment Trust (REIT): A Real estate Investment Trust is a legal entity that operates under a trust agreement rather than using articles of incorporation in order to gain favourable tax treatment. As its name indicates REITs invest primarily in real estate projects. Typically, they pay most of their cash-flow to their unitholders.

Research and Development (R&D): Research and development involves investigation and research with the intention to invent new products or processes or to improve old ones. When a firm prepares its financial reports, R&D will show up as a cost in the income statement, but it is hoped that it will eventually be translated into an asset (via patents) on the balance sheet.

Return on Invested Capital: Return on Invested Capital is the measure of net income as a percentage of all capital used by the company. This includes common shareholder's equity, preferred share equity and all debt.

Return on Equity: Return on Equity is net income divided by common shareholder's equity.

Reversion to the Mean: Stocks and stock markets tend to move up and down; some would say in random fashion. Unless a stock trades down to zero, at some point it will always revert to its average price over time.

Russian Debt Default: After emerging from behind the iron curtain in the 1980's, Russia encountered serious difficulties in the 1990's. The war in Chechnya was a costly and the country ran a huge governmental budget deficit. As well, it was stuck with a very unfavorable exchange rate between the ruble and the currencies of all its trading partners. Then came the Asian financial crisis and a crash in oil prices. On 17 August 1998, the Russian government devalued the ruble, defaulted on domestic debt, and declared a moratorium on repayment of foreign debt, creating havoc in capital markets around the globe.

S&P 500: The Standard & Poor's 500 Index is a capitalization-weighted index of 500 stocks. It is a much broader index than the Dow Jones Industrial Average, and is designed to measure the performance of the broad domestic equity market through changes in the aggregate market value of 500 stocks representing all major industries.

S&P-TSX Composite Index: The S&P-TSX Composite Index is the most recognized index of common stocks in Canada. It replaced the former TSE 300 Index in 199 when the Toronto Stock Exchange transferred management of the index to Standard and Poor's. The index now comprises about 240 stocks.

Securities Exchange Commission (SEC): The SEC is the agency within the US government that is responsible for regulating the US securities industry and for proposing securities laws as well as enforcing existing rules.

Segregated Fund: A segregated (seg) fund is a mutual fund wrapped up with an insurance policy. Seg funds offer many of the same benefits and pitfalls of mutual funds with a few added twists. For example, because they are connected to an insurance policy, they are insulated from creditors, should you ever go bankrupt. As well, so long as you have named a beneficiary, they are exempt from probate fees when you die.

Short-Selling: Short-selling is the sale of a security you do not own. It is facilitated by the brokerage firm lending the required security to the client doing the short-sale, and is done with the hope that the given security will trade down in price. The client then buys back the stock, returns it to the brokerage, and pockets the difference. A short-sale must be declared prior to making the transaction.

Speculating: Speculating is trading in an asset and taking on significant risk in the hopes of making a profit, often without sufficient evidence of the worthiness of the asset.

Standard Deviation: Standard deviation is a measure of volatility used in statistics, and it is how conventional wisdom defines risk. Not necessarily the odds of losing all your money, but rather the chances your rate of return will be something other than the average. So, if your return is above average, conventional wisdom is that it must be risky.

Statistics Canada: Statistics Canada is the Canadian federal government agency commissioned with producing statistics to help better understand Canada, its population, resources, economy, society, and culture. Its headquarters is in Ottawa.

Technical Analysis: Technical analysis tries to predict future movements in the price of a stock or the level of the market by studying where it has already been. The premise on which the technician bases his theory is that human behavior is predictable, and we tend to exhibit the same behavior (and make the same mistakes) time and time again. Technicians make extensive use of charts and graphs in their work.

Time Horizon: Your time horizon is a critical factor in deciding on how to structure your investments. It is the period of time you will be able to adhere to a given investment strategy without having to withdraw significant funds. If you have no near or intermediate term needs for the money you have invested, you are better able to assume the risk of a more volatile portfolio, knowing that if the market or a particular stock turns down temporarily, you will be able to wait it out, provided the long-term prospects are favorable.

Trailer Fees: Trailer fees are residuals paid by a mutual fund company to your broker or financial planner in return for the broker keeping you invested in their fund.

Underwriter: An underwriter is a brokerage or banking institution who funds and prepares the myriad of documents for taking a privately owned company to the market via an initial public offering, or helps an existing public company raise capital via a secondary offering. Depending on the size of the issue, there may be one or several underwriters involved in the process.

US Federal Reserve: The US Federal Reserve is the central bank in the United States; the largest economy in the world.

US Treasury Bonds: US Treasury Bonds are issued by the US Federal Reserve. These instruments normally pay interest at an agreed upon rate; twice a year. US Treasuries are issued for terms of more than one year.

Wholesaling: To engage in Real Estate Wholesaling is look for properties for which you believe the asking price is below the actual market value. Once you find your target property, you enter into a contract to purchase it, then immediately put it up for sale at a higher price.

Wrap Accounts: A wrap account is one in which a bank or broker manages an investor's portfolio for a flat annual fee. The investor usually completes a questionnaire and is then offered a portfolio consisting of several pooled funds. A pooled fund is similar to a mutual fund, except that it does not have a prospectus, is specifically designed for certain wrap accounts. and is not otherwise available to the general public.

About the Author

Before his retirement from active portfolio management in 2014, Bill Bignell spent more than 30 years in the investment industry. After working for three years as a Registered Representative for a large Canadian brokerage firm, he moved to The Canada Trust Company, where he helped launch a new division for the company managing personal investment accounts. During his tenure at Canada Trust Private Client Services, he managed upwards to $350 million. Bill moved to Bank of Montreal subsidiary BMO Harris Investment Management in 1998 to set up its investment operations in Mid-Western Ontario.

In 2000, Bill joined Leon Fraser & Associates (one of Canada's oldest independent asset managers) as Vice-President & Portfolio Manager. He transferred to sister company MGI Securities after seven years to set up MGI's managed portfolio division - taking on the role of Head Portfolio Manager.

Mr. Bignell holds a Bachelor's degree in Economics and Diploma in Business Administration from Wilfrid Laurier University in Waterloo Ontario, and a Masters Degree in Finance from the University of Leicester. As well, Bill earned the Certified Investment Manager and Certified Financial Planner designations, and before his retirement was a Fellow of the Canadian Securities Institute.

Author's note: My goals in writing this book were to illustrate that you don't have to be a genius to fare well in the stock market, to expose many of the mysteries that strike fear into the hearts of so many investors and to provide readers with a game plan they can use to make profitable investment decisions and enhance their portfolio returns.

I'd also like to sell a few books. So, if you like what you have read, I would be eternally grateful if you would tell your friends about it. They can buy a copy either as an e-book or hard-copy through Amazon.com at a very reasonable price.

And don't forget to leave a rating/review on Amazon!

Check out my website at www.marketbeater.ca
or email me at wbignell@marketbeater.ca

www.ingramcontent.com/pod-product-compliance
Lightning Source LLC
Chambersburg PA
CBHW070924210326
41520CB00021B/6800